THE DAILY ADVERTISER

OUR TEAM ⚜ OUR TIME

NEW ORLEANS SAINTS ▪ 2009 WORLD CHAMPIONS

And Dat's Dat!

THE DAILY ADVERTISER
theadvertiser.com

Leslie Hurst, *President and Publisher*

Published by Pediment Publishing, a division of The Pediment Group, Inc. www.pediment.com Printed in Canada

Foreword

By Kevin Foote

It was May 1974 and a 7-year-old boy sat, head lowered, at his father's wake. At such a young age, the boy couldn't understand the ramifications of everything that had just happened.

And he didn't try.

Just a few days before, the father who had introduced him to sports had been murdered, shot twice in the head while on his way to work.

At the wake, relatives stood helpless, not knowing what to say. How could they? What do you say to a 7-year-old who had just lost his father?

Finally, the boy's uncles fell back on the one subject — other than their unconditional love for one another — that united the family: the New Orleans Saints.

"So how do you think the Saints are going to do this year, Kevin?" they asked.

I don't remember my answer. And the truth is, it didn't matter.

In the have-and-have-nots NFL of that era, my uncles knew what the Saints were going to do. They had been 5-9 in 1973, and would be 5-9 during that 1974 season, too.

But it didn't matter. That was our team. They were the New Orleans Saints.

My father never knew who Chuck Muncie, Rickey Jackson, Bobby Hebert, William Roaf, Sammy Knight, Aaron Brooks, Tracy Porter or Drew Brees were. That was stolen by a gunman's bullet. But he knew how much fun it was to have an NFL franchise in New Orleans, and he understood hope.

The hope that one day it was going to happen. The hope that the franchise awarded to Louisiana — our franchise — actually could be the king of the NFL.

My father instilled that hope in me. He lit a flame of love and devotion for the Saints that went far beyond football.

The burning desire he instilled in me was his legacy.

As life continued to play out, that love and devotion for the Saints have been both a blessing and a curse.

I've missed valuable time with my own family by being completely captivated by the Saints game on TV. I deprived my mother the chance to watch her oldest son graduate from college. On Dec. 16, 1990, the day I was to graduate, I was covering the Saints' 9-6 loss to the Pittsburgh

Steelers in the Superdome. In my world, that was more important than attending a ceremony.

There have been many ups and downs over the years. But when Tracy Porter intercepted Peyton Manning and streaked 74 yards for a touchdown on the night of Feb. 7, 2010, so many of those heartbreaking moments in my love affair with the Saints disappeared. They just didn't matter anymore.

New Orleans Saints 31.

Indianapolis Colts 17.

World champions.

How sweet does that sound?

Who would have guessed back on May 17, 1974, that the Saints would win the Super Bowl before the crime was solved?

At long last, we have justice for die-hard Saints fans everywhere.

Acknowledgments

BOB HEIST
THE DAILY ADVERTISER
Sports Editor

BRADY AYMOND
THE DAILY ADVERTISER
Staff Writer

RICK CLEVELAND
THE CLARION LEDGER (MS)
Staff Writer

KEVIN FOOTE
THE DAILY ADVERTISER
Staff Writer

GLENN GUILBEAU
GANNETT LOUISIANA
Staff Writer

BOB TOMPKINS
THE TOWN TALK
Staff Writer

DENNY CULBERT
THE DAILY ADVERTISER
Staff photographer

BRAD KEMP
THE DAILY ADVERTISER
Staff Photographer

LESLIE WESTBROOK
THE DAILY ADVERTISER
Staff Photographer

CLAUDIA LAWS
THE DAILY ADVERTISER
Book Photo Editor

The Daily Advertiser would like to recognize the following sponsors:

Table of Contents

AN EARLY SURGE

THE FIRST HALF OF THE SEASON

By Brady Aymond

At the time, the play call seemed more about pride than anything else. But nobody knew how big the decision would turn out to be.

And fittingly enough, the call came at the site of Super Bowl XLIV, some 15 weeks earlier.

With the unbeaten New Orleans Saints losing to the Miami Dolphins, 24-3, and just five seconds remaining in the first half, coach Sean Payton

OPPOSITE: Quarterback Drew Brees drops back to pass in the first quarter against the Giants Sunday, Oct. 18, 2009, at the Superdome in New Orleans. New Orleans defeated New York 48-27. *Denny Culbert/The Daily Advertiser*

faced a decision.

The Saints were at the Dolphins' 1-yard line, courtesy of a Marques Colston 21-yard catch, which was initially ruled a touchdown but reversed after instant replay confirmed his knee was down before extending the ball past the goal line.

While the play was being reviewed, Payton stood on the sideline, ready to send the field goal unit onto the field. But quarterback Drew Brees had other plans.

He pleaded with Payton, imploring the coach to go for the touchdown.

"I told him I'd get it," Brees said. "I said, 'I'll get the touchdown. I know exactly what to do.' "

Payton gave in to Brees and the Saints offense marched back out. Brees called his own number, sneaking the ball across the goal line to cut the Dolphins' lead to 24-10.

No big deal, right?

Well, it was, as the Saints took that momentum and turned it into a 36-point outburst in the second half to race past the Dolphins, 46-34, to move to 6-0 and send a statement to the rest of the NFL.

"I know the Dolphins were ahead at halftime, but again, by the fourth quarter, they're running out the clock in that game," New England Patriots coach Bill Belichick would say later. "They're a strong, explosive team."

Through the first eight games, that was certainly the best description.

The Saints breezed through their first five games — dominating Detroit, 45-27, and pounding Philadelphia, 48-22, before taking a bite out of the Big Apple with a sweep of the Buffalo Bills, New York Jets and New York Giants.

Following the close win at Miami, the Saints beat division rivals Atlanta and Carolina in the Louisiana Superdome to open the season 8-0 for the first time in franchise history.

At the midway point, the Saints were averaging 37.9 points per game and winning by an average of 16 points.

Little did they know, the best was yet to come. ✣

SEPTEMBER 13, 2009

WEEK 1
Saints vs. Lions
W 45-27

ABOVE: Saints wide receiver Marques Colston battles defender Eric King during the win over Detroit at the Louisiana Superdome in New Orleans. *Denny Culbert/The Daily Advertiser*

RIGHT: Saints quarterback Drew Brees throws the ball downfield. *Denny Culbert/ The Daily Advertiser*

OPPOSITE: Saints defensive tackle Sedrick Ellis attempts to block a pass. *Denny Culbert/The Daily Advertiser*

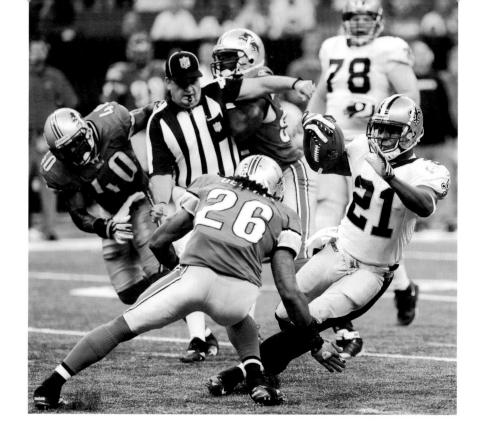

ABOVE: Saints wide receiver Devery Henderson, left, is congratulated by Jeremy Shockey after a key running play against the Lions. *Denny Culbert/The Daily Advertiser*

TOP LEFT: Running back Mike Bell tries to avoid Lions defender Louis Delmas. *Denny Culbert/The Daily Advertiser*

LEFT: Saints wide receiver Devery Henderson gains yardage against the Lions. *Denny Culbert/The Daily Advertiser*

FAR LEFT: Detroit's Marquand Manuel attempts to block a pass to wide receiver Devery Henderson. *Denny Culbert/The Daily Advertiser*

OPPOSITE: Saints running back Reggie Bush makes a drive against the Lions. *Denny Culbert/The Daily Advertiser*

SEPTEMBER 20, 2009

WEEK 2

Saints vs. Eagles

W 48-22

BestBets

Baseball Inside

Fielder powers Brewers to sweep of Astros

Prince Fielder hit his 40th homer and set a franchise record with his 127th RBI as the Milwaukee Brewers beat the Houston Astros, 6-0, on Sunday to finish off a three-game sweep.

MLB Roundup ▸ Page 2B

Sports in brief

Martin grabs 5th win in season in Chase opener

LOUDON, N.H. — **Mark Martin** held off **Juan Pablo Montoya** on a late frantic restart to win the Chase for the Sprint Cup championship opener at New Hampshire Motor Speedway.

It is Martin's series-best fifth victory of the season and spoiled what could have been a blockbuster day for Montoya. Making his 100th career start on his 34th birthday, Montoya led every practice session while setting the stage for his second career Sprint Cup Series victory.

Instead, Martin used pit strategy to take the lead, and after leading a race-high 104 laps, Montoya had to chase him down.

He came up short in a three-lap sprint to the finish, which ended under caution when **AJ Allmendinger** wrecked.

NASCAR said **Denny Hamlin** was ahead of Montoya when the caution came up, and was given second place in the finishing order. Montoya was third.

Three-time defending series champion **Jimmie Johnson** was fourth, and **Kyle Busch**, who missed making the Chase by just eight points, rounded out the top five finishers.

Kurt Busch was sixth and followed by Ryan Newman, Elliott Sadler, defending race winner Greg Biffle and Clint Bowyer.

New College Rankings

Associated Press Top 10

Team	Record	Pvs
1. Florida	3-0	1
2. Texas	3-0	2
3. Alabama	3-0	4
4. Ole Miss	2-0	5
5. Penn St.	3-0	5
6. California	3-0	6
7. LSU	3-0	9
8. Boise St.	3-0	10
9. Miami	2-0	9
10. Oklahoma	2-1	12

Complete Polls ▸ Page 2B

Only on the Web

UL Blog

Daily Advertiser writer **Joshua Parrott** keeps fans of Ragin' Cajuns athletics up to date with all things UL with his daily blog.

For those features and more, go to theadvertiser.com.

Get breaking sports on your cell phone

Sign up at the advertiser.com/textme

GetPublished

Share your news, photos and events

E-mail: sports@theadvertiser.com
Call: 289-6300
Fax: 371-3341
Mail: The Daily Advertiser
1100 Bertrand Drive
Lafayette, LA 70506

No denying effort

Missed chances hurt UL's shot at win

Joshua Parrott
jparrott@theadvertiser.com

BATON ROUGE — The hurt felt in UL's locker room after a 31-3 loss Saturday night to No. 9 LSU was visible on the faces of Ragin' Cajun players and coaches.

Chris Fisher showed the pain in a brief post-game interview. Forgetting the entire experience, he says, would be a huge mistake for the program — which refuses to take a moral victory from the loss.

"I don't want to flush the whole thing," said the senior center from Lafayette.

"If you do that, you're acting like it never happened, and I don't think we should do that. I saw good effort and everybody playing for each other, trying to do everything they could to win the game.

See UL on Page 3B

What's up next

Ragin' Cajuns (2-1) at No. 25 Nebraska (2-1)
Memorial Stadium
Lincoln, Neb.
Saturday • 6 p.m.

A failed opportunity on a fourth-down run at the goal line by Undrea Sails in the third quarter kept UL from possibly drawing within 24-10 of LSU on Saturday night in Tiger Stadium.

Leslie Westbrook / lwestbrook@theadvertiser.com

SAINTS 48 • EAGLES 22

2-AND-OH!

ANOTHER AIR STRIKE
The Eagles were no match for a passing game that put up 311 yards and 3 TDs.

DEFENSE STATES CASE
The Saints limited the Eagles to 85 yards rushing and created four turnovers.

New Orleans Saints wide receiver Marques Colston pulls in a touchdown pass in front of Philadelphia Eagles cornerback Asante Samuel during the first quarter of Sunday's game at Lincoln Financial Field in Philadelphia. Colston caught eight balls for 98 yards and a pair of scores as the Saints rolled up more than 400 yards of offense in a 48-22 win.

The Associated Press

Saints remain perfect as offense overwhelms Philly

The Associated Press

PHILADELPHIA — Without Donovan McNabb, the Philadelphia Eagles tried everything they could on offense. Drew Brees and the New Orleans Saints stuck to what they do best.

Brees tossed three more touchdown passes on Sunday, helping the Saints beat Philadelphia, 48-22.

Brees had six TD passes last week as the Saints (2-0) routed Detroit, 45-27. He picked up where he left off, picking apart Philadelphia's secondary and completing 25 of 34 passes for 311 yards and one interception.

"If you look at our skill group, each game no guy ever knows who's day it's gonna be," Brees said. "Each guy knows it's their job to open things up for everyone else."

Making his first NFL start for an injured McNabb, Kevin Kolb threw for 391 yards and two TDs, including a 71-yard scoring pass to DeSean Jackson. Kolb also threw three interceptions, though, including one returned 97 yards for a TD by Darren Sharper in the final minute.

"I've got to cut those turnovers out," Kolb said. "I know better than that. I will do it."

McNabb sat out with a cracked rib. With the five-time Pro Bowl QB in street clothes, the Eagles (1-1) showed off their creativity on offense.

Coach Andy Reid and offensive coordinator Marty Mornhinweg used several variations of the wildcat formation with three different players taking snaps. Both tackles were split wide one time

See SAINTS on Page 5B

More NFL Inside

STATS & FACTS
Find complete game statistics and capsules, breaking news and the top performers from Sunday on the weekly review page for the NFL.

NFL Blitz ▸ Page 4B

Brees
Leading the NFL with a total of nine TD passes.

IT'S BEEN ALL THUMBS UP FOR THE SAINTS AFTER TWO GAMES

A STRONG BREES
After two outstanding games, Saints QB Drew Brees has passed for 669 yards and 9 TDs in 2009.

MISSING LINK
Darren Sharper has helped plug a leaky secondary with 2 INTs, one returned 97 yards for a TD Sunday.

PINBALL OFFENSE
The Saints have been awesome, averaging 468 yards of total offense and 46.5 points per game.

Glenn Guilbeau
gguilbeau@gannett.com

Ranking teams clearly not an exact science

No one is really that good at ranking college football teams.

It can be a very difficult thing to do, but since no one is really that good at it, just about anyone with a strong interest in college football can do it.

I have voted in The Associated Press poll for the last three seasons and also voted in it during the early 1990s. I enjoy doing it mainly because when I was a kid I never could understand how certain voting took place.

For example, I often noticed and still notice how a team that had beaten another team and had a similar record was not ranked ahead of that team. This happened in the final poll last season when Georgia Tech finished at No. 22 with a 9-4 record. LSU had just destroyed Tech, 38-3, in the Chick-fil-A Bowl to finish 8-5, but Tech stayed ranked and LSU didn't make the poll.

What gives? Voters just figured Tech deserved a Christmas vacation? Is 9-4 that much better than 8-5?

Similar things appear in today's AP poll. For example, Washington is 1-2-1 and beat USC, which is 2-1, but Washington is ranked No. 34 and USC is No. 12. Yes, USC was ranked No. 3, but that should not matter this early in the season. Washington beat USC.

Sure, if a 2-6 team upsets a 9-1 team that is No. 3 in the nation then, yes, the 3-8 team would not get ranked higher than the 9-2 team.

But Washington also played a very good game against LSU, which is ranked No. 7 today.

So why does USC stay ahead of a team it just lost to in so freakish way whatsoever? What, did Washington have a career night, and USC had the flu?

Here's another example. Unranked Houston upset No. 5 Oklahoma State back in week two, 45-35, and was off over the weekend. Houston is 2-0. Oklahoma State is 2-1, but Oklahoma State is No. 18.

See GUILBEAU on Page 3B

LSU Football Inside

DEFENSE IMPROVING
After standing last in the SEC in total defense after the first game at Washington, LSU has risen to No. 9 in the nation.

Notebook ▸ Page 3B

1B **Sports**

2009 GMC SIERRA 1500 EXTENDED CAB
MSRP $29,260
REBATE $4,000
60 DAY GUARANTEE WAIVER REBATE $500
DEALER DISCOUNT $3,772
SELLING PRICE PLUS T.T.L. $20,988
4750 JOHNSTON STREET, LAFAYETTE
COURTESY 337-984-1GMC

Monday, September 28, 2009 | theadvertiser.com | The Advertiser

BestBets

NFL inside

Lions snap 19-game losing skid with win over Skins

Rookie quarterback **Matthew Stafford** threw for 241 yards and a touchdown as the Detroit Lions picked up their first regular season win since Dec. 23, 2007, with a 19-14 victory.

NFL Blitz • Page 3B

Sports in brief

Florida's Tebow home after night in hospital

GAINESVILLE, Fla. — Florida quarterback **Tim Tebow** is back home after spending the night in the hospital with a concussion. How long before he plays again is now the big question facing the Gators.

Tebow

Tebow was released from a Lexington, Ky., hospital Sunday morning, about 12 hours after sustaining a concussion in the Gators' 41-7 victory at Kentucky. He was held for precautionary reasons and tests.

"Tim is doing fine this morning," said coach **Urban Meyer**, who stayed behind with Tebow. "His CT scans came back and indicated that Tim suffered a concussion. Our medical and athletic training staff will continue to monitor him to determine how much rest and recovery he needs. We will have additional information and updates this week."

Tebow flew back to Gainesville with Meyer and his family Sunday afternoon.

The top-ranked Gators (4-0) are off next week, then play at LSU on Oct. 10. It might be several days, maybe longer, before Tebow's status becomes clearer for what could be the toughest game on the defending national champions' schedule.

New College Rankings

Associated Press Top 10

Team	Record	Pvs
1. Florida	4-0	1
2. Texas	4-0	2
3. Alabama	4-0	3
4. LSU	**4-0**	**7**
5. Boise State	4-0	8
6. Virginia Tech	3-1	11
7. USC	3-1	12
8. Oklahoma	2-1	10
9. Ohio State	3-1	13
10. Cincinnati	4-0	14

Complete Polls • Page 2B

Only on the Web

UL Blog

Daily Advertiser writer **Joshua Parrott** keeps fans of Ragin' Cajuns athletics up to date with all things UL with his daily blog.

For these features and more, go to theadvertiser.com.

Get breaking sports on your cell phone
Sign up @theadvertiser.com/textme

GetPublished

Share your news, photos and events

E-mail: sports@theadvertiser.com
Call: 289-6303
Fax: 371-3341
Mail: The Daily Advertiser
1100 Bertrand Drive
Lafayette, LA 70506

UL bye week comes at perfect time

Players will use break to recover from injuries

Bustie
Says bye week will be 'incredible' for Cajuns.

Joshua Parrott
jparrott@theadvertiser.com

LINCOLN, Neb. — The first bye week of the season for UL arrives at a perfect time.

After playing four consecutive games, including the past three against BCS conference teams, the Ragin' Cajuns need a chance to recover. They are bruised, battered and beaten up. Some players have spent more time in the athletic training room than on the field.

More inside
HUSKERS OFFENSE
■ UL struggled against Nebraska playmakers Saturday.
Story • Page 4D

Head coach Rickey Bustie estimated that nine players sat out last Saturday's 55-0 loss at then-No. 25 Nebraska because of injury. Among the sidelined players were UL's top four safeties, all-Sun Belt Conference center Chris Fisher and receiver Richie Falgout.

At least four other players got hurt in the first

See UL on Page 4B

The Associated Press
UL's Brad McGuire is tackled by Nebraska's Matt O'Hanlon (33) in the second half of their game Saturday.

27 7

Marching on

Photos by The Associated Press
New Orleans Saints running back Pierre Thomas (23) runs past Buffalo Bills linebacker Keith Ellison (56) for a fourth-quarter touchdown Sunday. Thomas came off the bench in the second half to rush for 126 yards.

Saints' defense paves the way as team improves to 3-0 with win over Buffalo

The Associated Press

ORCHARD PARK, N.Y. — Turns out Drew Brees doesn't have to throw a touchdown pass — or put up 45 points — to secure a victory.

The New Orleans Saints' overlooked defense proved pretty stout.

Will Smith had a sack and an interception to lead a Saints defense that held Terrell Owens without a catch for the first time since his rookie season in 1996 on the way to New Orleans' 27-7 win over the Buffalo Bills on Sunday.

Running back Pierre Thomas sealed the win by scoring two touchdowns in the final 10 minutes and finished with a career-high 126 yards rushing — all in the second half.

Brees finished 16 of 20 for 172 yards, ending an NFL-leading 22-game streak of throwing for 200 yards or more.

"Our defense played outstanding," Brees said. "Every time they stepped on the field, they just felt like they were going to shut them down."

See SAINTS on Page 2B

New Orleans Saints running back Pierre Thomas, left, and teammate Jahri Evans celebrate Thomas' fourth-quarter touchdown against the Buffalo Bills.

By the numbers

0 The Saints held Buffalo without a first down in the entire fourth quarter.

97 The Saints held Fred Jackson to only 97 yards of total offense on 22 touches.

9.0 Pierre Thomas averaged nearly 10 yards a carry for the Saints on Sunday.

14% The Saints' defense got off the field on third down, holding Buffalo to 2-of-14.

185 Terrell Owens was held without a catch for the first time in 185 career games.

Glenn Guilbeau
gguilbeau@gannett.com

I do believe what I just didn't see

BATON ROUGE — It never ceases to amaze me how the closer someone is to a football game, the less they see.

Davis Wade Stadium, site of LSU's 30-26 victory over Mississippi State on Saturday in Starkville, Miss., has a huge video board the size of a classic drive-in theater screen. It dwarfs the actual live action on the field. You could almost watch a game in Starkville from Tupelo and not worry about which of the 16 ESPN channels it may be on. Instead of buying a satellite ... watch the big space ship.

The actual game seemed like a miniature model, only with moving parts.

Davis Wade is not a very large stadium either. It seats only 55,082, so there are no seats in heaven as in Tiger Stadium. In other words, it's hard to miss a play at Davis Wade.

But that fourth-and-goal play by Mississippi State with just over a minute to play Saturday that decided the game, just about everyone missed it.

"The very last play? I did not see it," said Les Miles, who coaches the LSU football team usually from about the 50.

"I saw the quarterback on the triple option find that there was a deep penetration in about the B gap. He planted north and south, and that's where I lost sight of the ball from the sidelines."

What everybody saw was State quarterback Tyson Lee disappear into the belly of the LSU defense. Then he resurfaced and tried to inch into the end zone, but LSU safety Chad Jones finished him off at the top.

Jones is a crafty, left-handed, set-up relief pitcher with a nasty slider on the baseball team, but that was the first save of his career. Everybody saw that.

But no one could tell who had Lee from the bottom. Even on the many ESPN replays, Lee just looked like he was in purple goo. No one could make out a number.

"Drake Nevis, the tackle, hit him first," someone said in the pressbox, and suddenly that was the consensus.

Until Nevis spoke to reporters on the field after

See GUILBEAU on Page 4B

FOR HOME DELIVERY, CALL 800-259-8852

SEPTEMBER 27, 2009

WEEK 3

Saints vs. Bills

W 27-7

LEFT: A Saints fan shows off her muscle during the NFC divisional playoff game between the New Orleans Saints and the Arizona Cardinals Saturday, January 16, 2010, at the Superdome in New Orleans. *Leslie Westbrook/The Daily Advertiser*

OPPOSITE: Saints fans support their team in a win over the Cardinals Saturday, January 16, 2010, at the Superdome in New Orleans. The Saints defeated the Cardinals 45-14 in their NFC divisional playoff game. *Denny Culbert/The Daily Advertiser*

RIGHT: Randall Gay celebrates his interception to ice the game against the Jets. *Brad Kemp/The Daily Advertiser*

FAR TOP RIGHT: Wide receiver Robert Meachem just misses the ball while being defended by the Jets' Dwight Lowery. *Brad Kemp/The Daily Advertiser*

FAR MIDDLE RIGHT: Darren Sharper tackles Dustin Keller during the Saints' win, 24-10. *Brad Kemp/The Daily Advertiser*

FAR BOTTOM RIGHT: Reggie Bush avoids the Jets defense as he gains rushing yards. *Brad Kemp/The Daily Advertiser*

OPPOSITE: New Orleans Saints Pierre Thomas breaks the tackle of the Jets' Dwight Lowery. *Brad Kemp/The Daily Advertiser*

PREVIOUS LEFT: The Saints' Jonathan Casillas, from left, Anthony Hargrove and Chris Reis celebrate during the 24-10 win over the Jets. *Brad Kemp/The Daily Advertiser*

PREVIOUS MIDDLE: Pierre Thomas breaks the tackle of Dwight Lowery. *Brad Kemp/The Daily Advertiser*

PREVIOUS TOP RIGHT: Saints Lance Moore dives for more yardage against the Jets' Drew Coleman during the game at the Superdome. *Brad Kemp/The Daily Advertiser*

PREVIOUS BOTTOM LEFT: Pierre Thomas goes in for a score against the Jets. *Brad Kemp/The Daily Advertiser*

PREVIOUS BOTTOM RIGHT: Jets Thomas Jones, center, is tackled by Saints players Bobby McCray (93), Scott Fujita (55) and Roman Harper (41). *Brad Kemp/The Daily Advertiser*

ABOVE: Head coach Sean Payton calls a play during the game against the Giants at the Superdome in New Orleans.
Denny Culbert/The Daily Advertiser

RIGHT: Wide receiver Lance Moore battles Giants defender Aaron Rouse.
Denny Culbert/The Daily Advertiser

OPPOSITE: Wide receiver Courtney Roby makes his way through the Giants defense.
Denny Culbert/The Daily Advertiser

BestBets

Web Extra

Reflections on UL's win at Western Kentucky
UL's Devon Lewis-Buchanan, top, tackles Western Kentucky's Dexter Taylor during Saturday night's game. Cajuns beat writer Joshua Parrott gives his take on the contest in Bowling Green, Ky., won by UL, 30-22, to move to 2-0 in the Sun Belt Conference.
www.theadvertiser.com

Sports in brief

Lee dominates Dodgers; Phils romp for 2-1 lead

PHILADELPHIA — Cliff Lee dominated the Dodgers, Ryan Howard and Jayson Werth provided the big swings early and the Philadelphia Phillies cruised past Los Angeles 11-0 Sunday night for a 2-1 lead in the NL championship series.

Lee provided another brilliant playoff start, striking out 10 and allowing only three hits in eight innings.

Howard hustled for a triple, Werth homered and the Phillies led 6-0 by the second inning. Howard made two headfirst dives during the romp — the big slugger has an RBI in all seven of Philadelphia's playoff games this year, a record streak in a single postseason.

Coming off the most lopsided win in their postseason history, the defending World Series champion Phillies will try to move closer to a return in Game 4 tonight. Joe Blanton starts against the Dodgers' Randy Wolf, who hasn't pitched since the opener of the division series against St. Louis.

Howard had three RBIs, including his two-run triple in the first. Werth followed that with a two-run homer, and that was more than enough for Lee.

The reigning AL Cy Young Award winner faced just two batters over the minimum. Lee gave up a pair of singles to Manny Ramirez and one to Ronnie Belliard.

Lee is 2-0 with an 0.74 ERA in three postseason starts, giving the Phillies exactly what they expected when they acquired him from Cleveland in late July.

Boxscore ▸ Page 2B

New College Rankings
Associated Press Top 10

Team	Record	Pvs
1. Alabama	7-0	2
2. Florida	6-0	1
3. Texas	6-0	3
4. Southern Cal	5-1	6
5. Cincinnati	6-0	8
6. Boise St.	6-0	5
7. Iowa	7-0	11
8. Miami	5-1	9
9. LSU	5-1	10
10. TCU	6-0	12

Complete Polls ▸ Page 2B

Only on the Web

UL Blog
Daily Advertiser writer Joshua Parrott keeps fans of Ragin' Cajuns athletics up to date with all things UL with his daily blog.

For these features and more, go to theadvertiser.com.

GetPublished

Share your news, photos and events

E-mail: sports@theadvertiser.com
Call: 289-6303
Fax: 371-3341
Mail: The Daily Advertiser
1100 Bertrand Drive
Lafayette, LA 70506

 48 —  27

LOWERING THE BOOM

Mike Bell's 2-yard touchdown run was the first by seven different players for the Saints in the landslide victory.

Saints take giant step with blowout win

Glenn Guilbeau
gguilbeau@gannett.com

'They're Off!' and running in Big Easy

NEW ORLEANS — The Fair Grounds track doesn't open its 138th season of horse racing here until Nov. 6.

But New Orleans tight end Jeremy Shockey decided to say, "And they're off!" a few weeks early Sunday afternoon in the Superdome as he helped start the Saints' 48-27 trampling of the previously undefeated New York Giants, who are also his former team.

After catching a 1-yard touchdown to give the Saints a 14-0 lead less than 13 minutes out of the gate, he hopped on a make-believe horse, struck it with his make-believe whip and rode off into the sunset. Well, actually it was to the sideline to adoring teammates and coaches — something Shockey didn't always have in New York.

Technically, the Saints were not yet in the winner's circle, but in reality it was over. The Giants never knew what ran over them.

"Yeah, I was shocked," New York linebacker Antonio Pierce said. "I didn't see 48 points and four touchdowns against a defense that rode into the dome No. 1 in the NFL in pass defense with a mere 104.8 yards allowed. Brees threw for 123 in the first quarter alone. The Saints nearly put half a thousand on the NFL's No. 1 unit in total defense with 210 allowed. Seven players scored touchdowns.

Every time you looked up, the Saints were scoring a touchdown. New York quarterback Eli Manning, an old Shockey nemesis who was 14 of 31 for 178 yards with an interception, now knows what his dad, Archie, went

See GUILBEAU on Page 2B

New Orleans Saints wide receiver Lance Moore (16) celebrates his 12-yard touchdown catch with teammate Reggie Bush during the second quarter of Sunday's game against the New York Giants in the Louisiana Superdome. In a showdown of unbeaten teams, the Saints overpowered the Giants, piling up nearly 500 yards of offense during a lopsided 48-27 victory.
Denny Culbert / dculbert@theadvertiser.com

Brady Aymond
baymond@theadvertiser.com

NEW ORLEANS — The showdown turned into a beatdown.

Beauty beat brawn. Brees beat Manning.

And the unbeaten New Orleans Saints beat up the previously unbeaten New York Giants.

And just like that, the rest of the NFC was put on notice — the Saints have risen to contender status.

Drew Brees shredded the NFL's top defense for 369 passing yards — 264 yards more than their league-best average — as the Saints (5-0) rolled to a shockingly easy 48-27 win over the Giants on Sunday before a packed house of 70,011 in the Louisiana Superdome.

The Giants (5-1) entered the game with the NFL's top overall defense (210.6 yards

Brees
Went 23-of-30 for 369 yards and four TDs.

Coleston
Exploded for 8 catches, 166 yards, 1 TD.

per game) and top passing defense (104.8 yards per game).

"I felt like our preparation was great and that was a big difference," said Brees, who completed his first 15 passes and finished 23 of 30 with four touchdowns. "Number two, just the fact that you have the 5-0 Giants coming into town, a team that won the Super Bowl two years ago, was the first seed in the playoffs last year.

"They know the formula to win and the challenge for us was to play a team like this in our home stadium. What can I say? Everybody showed up. The fans were awesome. The defense played great. On offense, we did what we had to do."

And the Saints beat the Giants at their own game.

See SAINTS on Page 3B

More coverage inside

DEBUT & DUD
■ Just like his dad's first regular-season game in the Superdome, Eli Manning's debut was a complete dud.
Story ▸ Page 2B

POINT OF ATTACK
■ The Saints' offensive line dominated the point of attack against the NFL's top defense.
Story ▸ Page 3B

WEEK 6 SCOREBOARD

Green Bay	26	Houston	28	Carolina	28	Minnesota	33	Oakland	13	New England	59
Detroit	0	Cincinnati	17	Tampa Bay	21	Baltimore	31	Philadelphia		Tennessee	0
Pittsburgh	27	Kansas City	14	Jacksonville	23	Arizona	27	Buffalo	16	Atlanta	21
Cleveland	14	Washington	6	St. Louis	3	N.Y. Jets	20	Seattle		Chicago	14

LEFT: Saints wide receiver Marques Colston comes down with a pass on the one yard line in the first quarter. *Denny Culbert/ The Daily Advertiser*

OPPOSITE LEFT: Saints wide receiver Lance Moore celebrates after catching a touchdown pass in the second quarter against the Giants. *Denny Culbert/The Daily Advertiser*

OPPOSITE TOP RIGHT: Saints cornerback Malcolm Jenkins dives for Domenik Hixon during the win over the Giants. *Denny Culbert/The Daily Advertiser*

OPPOSITE MIDDLE RIGHT: Saints cornerback Jabari Greer breaks up a pass to Giants wide receiver Domenik Hixon in the first quarter. *Denny Culbert/The Daily Advertiser*

OPPOSITE BOTTOM RIGHT: Saints free safety Darren Sharper forces Mario Manningham to drop the ball during the Saints' 48-27 win. *Denny Culbert/The Daily Advertiser*

FOLLOWING LEFT: Saints cornerback Jabari Greer carries the ball after an interception in the third quarter. *Denny Culbert/ The Daily Advertiser*

FOLLOWING RIGHT: Saints safety Roman Harper rushes Giants quarterback Eli Manning in the first quarter. *Denny Culbert/ The Daily Advertiser*

LEFT: Saints fans cheer their team to a 48-27 win over the Giants. *Denny Culbert/ The Daily Advertiser*

BOTTOM LEFT: Tight end Jeremy Shockey looks to the crowd during the win. *Denny Culbert/The Daily Advertiser*

OPPOSITE: Quarterback Drew Brees waits on the sidelines. *Denny Culbert/ The Daily Advertiser*

BELOW: Running back Pierre Thomas gains yardage for the Saints against the Giants. *Denny Culbert/The Daily Advertiser*

1B | # Sports

Monday, October 26, 2009 · theadvertiser.com · The Advertiser

BestBets

Baseball Playoffs Inside

Yankees beat Angels for spot in the World Series

Johnny Damon's two-run single sparked a three-run fourth inning for the New York Yankees on Sunday night in Game 6 of the ALCS. The Yankees went on to beat the Los Angeles Angels, 5-2, for a spot in the World Series opposite the Philadelphia Phillies.

Story → Page 2B

Sports in brief

Mullen: SEC replay official blew call against Florida

JACKSON, Miss. — Mississippi State coach Dan Mullen called for disciplinary action against the Southeastern Conference replay official who worked the Bulldogs' 29-19 loss to Florida after a Gators touchdown that might have been a fumble was not overturned.

Mullen

Mullen said Sunday it's understandable if a field official makes a mistake because of the speed of the game, but the replay official can take his time and should be held accountable.

"I don't even know why we have replay right now in the Southeastern Conference if they're not going to utilize it," Mullen said.

"That's twice now that they've blown calls on the replay with our games, resulting in big plays, and I think that's unexcusable for that official. I hope he's severely punished if he ever works another or SEC game again, because I think it's completely unacceptable."

Mullen's comments come a few days after SEC commissioner Mike Slive suspended an officiating crew for two personal-foul penalties in the Arkansas-Florida and LSU-Georgia games that league officials said should not have been called.

It was the first time the league publicly suspended an officiating crew. The group won't return to duty till Nov. 14 and bowl assignments could be affected.

New College Rankings

Associated Press Top 10

Team	Record	Pvs
1. Florida	7-0	2
2. Alabama	8-0	1
3. Texas	8-0	3
4. Southern Cal	6-1	4
5. Cincinnati	7-0	5
6. Boise St.	7-0	6
7. Iowa	8-0	7
8. TCU	7-0	10
9. LSU	6-1	9
10. Oregon	6-1	12

Complete Polls → Page 2B

Only on the Web

UL Blog

Daily Advertiser writer Joshua Parrott keeps fans of Ragin' Cajuns athletics up to date with all things UL with his daily blog.

For these features and more, go to theadvertiser.com.

GetPublished

Share your news, photos and events

E-mail: sports@theadvertiser.com
Call: 289-6303
Fax: 371-3341
Mail: The Daily Advertiser
1100 Bertrand Drive
Lafayette, LA 70506

Plenty of areas remain for UL to improve

Joshua Parrott
jparrott@TheAdvertiser.com

Still counting up the slew of missed tackles that punctuated UL's 51-29 loss to Florida Atlantic on Saturday in Sun Belt Conference action at Cajun Field.

But that is just one of the areas of interest when looking back on the loss.

While some are coming down hard on the coaches, notably head coach Rickey Bustle, let's take a step back for a second.

Cornerback Dwight Bentley said himself that the Ragin' Cajun players lacked focus. There's no arguing that.

Missed tackles, blown assignments, sloppy effort — it all resulted in FAU rolling up a school-record 624 yards.

That's on the players, and they know it. So put away the pitchforks and re-channel your anger.

Obviously, the Cajuns did a terrible job of wrapping up and tackling. It was a poor defensive performance against an Owls team that has a history of taking advantage of mistakes.

There was no pass rush to be seen — again — as FAU quarterback Rusty Smith picked apart UL's soft zone for 359 yards and four scores. Two of his touchdown passes went to wide receiver Chris Bonner, who slipped past defenders for scoring receptions of 70 and 64 yards, respectively.

FAU tailback Alfred Morris, the Sun Belt's leading rusher, played like it with a career-high 181 yards and two touchdowns. On several plays, he picked up chunks of yardage after contact as defenders tried to strip the ball instead of bringing him down.

UL defensive coordinator Kevin Fouquier said the coaches need to figure out what they can

See UL on Page 4B

The Associated Press

Drew Brees goes over the top of his offensive line for a critical touchdown with two seconds to play before halftime of Sunday's game in Miami. Brees rushed for two short touchdowns and passed for another as the Saints mounted a brilliant second-half comeback to rally from a big deficit for a 46-34 win over the Dolphins and improve to 6-0 on the season.

LSU REWIND

Shepard gets his shot for spotlight

Glenn Guilbeau
gguilbeau@gannett.com

BATON ROUGE — Russell Shepard loves talking about his game nearly as much as playing his game.

"Holler at me," the true freshman said with a pretend phone at his ear to a member of LSU's sports information department a few days after his first piece of action as a Tiger. That was against Vanderbilt in week two and all he did was gain 27 yards on three carries, but he wanted to be interviewed.

LSU's sports information office was not ready at the time to bend LSU coach Les Miles' policy concerning freshmen, which prohibits interviews unless one does something significant in a game.

That finally happened Saturday night as Shepard sprinted 69 yards for a touchdown and was LSU's leading rusher with 71 yards on six carries during a 31-10 win over Auburn at Tiger Stadium.

"Any time a freshman has an impact on the game like that, I get with coach and ask if it's all right, and he was all for it," LSU sports information director Michael Bonnette said Sunday night. "Russell deserved the right. He was excited about the chance, and he did a nice job."

Shepard jumped at the media opportunity the same way he flew through the hole between left guard and left tackle for his touchdown.

"It was an amazing thing," Shepard said to a few reporters and television cameras. "It was kind of crazy because I scored by the student

See SHEPARD on Page 2B

Did you know?

FINALLY, A RUSHING TD

Jordan Jefferson's 15-yard TD run that gave the Tigers a 14-0 lead in the first quarter Saturday was the first rushing TD against Auburn for LSU since 2003.

Acadiana High grad Alley Broussard scored the previous rushing TD on a 5-yard run in LSU's 31-7 win in 2003.

South Beach Blitz

Saints explode for 36 points in second half to rally past Miami

The Associated Press

MIAMI — Drew Brees emerged from the locker room with a fresh cut under his chin and another between his eyebrows.

He made the Miami Dolphins look worse.

Brees and the unbeaten New Orleans Saints fell behind for the first time all season, then overcame a 21-point deficit Sunday to beat Miami, 46-34.

The NFL's highest-scoring team topped 40 points for the fourth time and outscored the Dolphins 22-0 in the fourth quarter.

"There was no doubt on our sideline we would come back and win," said Brees, who threw for 298 yards. "They had given us their best shot, and we had played about as bad as we could play. All we

Brees
Accounted for three scores on Sunday.

Sharper
INT return in Miami was third in 2009.

More NFL inside

STATS & FACTS
■ Find complete game stats and capsules, breaking news and the top performers from Sunday on the weekly review page for the NFL.

NFL Blitz → Page 5B

had to do was string together a few drives and gain the momentum back. We knew it was going to happen, and it did."

NFL passing leader Brees had his worst day of the season, with three interceptions and two fumble and two sacks. But he led touchdown drives of 82, 79 and 60 yards on successive possessions in the second half to put New Orleans ahead.

Brees threw for one touchdown and scored twice. After his 3-yard keeper with 8:35 left gave the Saints their first lead, he celebrated by dunking the ball over the crossbar.

"There are times in the game when a team just needs an emotional lift," he said. "I felt like I had to do something to get everybody hyped. The first thing that came to mind was to dunk it."

Fading at the finish, the Dolphins (2-4) couldn't handle the comeback.

interception return then sealed the win for the Saints (6-0), who are off to their best start since 1991 and are the only unbeaten team in the NFC.

"It can be a season-defining win," linebacker Scott Shanle said. "This was a test we hadn't faced yet, and we couldn't be happier with the way we responded."

Tracy Porter's 54-yard in-

See SAINTS on Page 4B

WEEK 7 SCOREBOARD

New England	35	Houston	24	San Diego	37	Buffalo	20	Dallas
Tampa Bay	7	San Francisco	21	Kansas City	7	Carolina	9	Atlanta
Pittsburgh	27	Indianapolis	42	Green Bay	31	N.Y. Jets	38	Cincinnati
Minnesota	17	St. Louis	6	Cleveland	3	Oakland	0	Chicago

| New Orleans | 46 |
| Miami | 34 |

| Arizona | 24 |
| N.Y. Giants | 17 |

NOVEMBER 2, 2009
WEEK 8
**Saints
vs. Falcons**

W 35-27

PREVIOUS LEFT: Atlanta Falcons running back Michael Turner (33) is brought down by Saints defenders Tracy Porter (22), Jo-Lonn Dunbar (56), and Scott Shanle (58). *Leslie Westbrook/The Daily Advertiser*

PREVIOUS RIGHT: New Orleans Saints wide receiver Marques Colston makes a leaping touchdown catch as Atlanta Falcons cornerback Tye Hill attempts to strip the ball. *Leslie Westbrook/The Daily Advertiser*

RIGHT: An official attempts to break up a skirmish between Saints tackle Jermon Bushrod and Falcons linebacker Stephen Nicholas. *Leslie Westbrook/The Daily Advertiser*

BOTTOM RIGHT: Saints cornerback Tracy Porter (22) tackles Atlanta Falcons tight end Tony Gonzalez (88). *Leslie Westbrook/ The Daily Advertiser*

OPPOSITE: Saints running back Mike Bell charges through the line. *Leslie Westbrook/ The Daily Advertiser*

BELOW: A fan holds up a sign. *Leslie Westbrook/The Daily Advertiser*

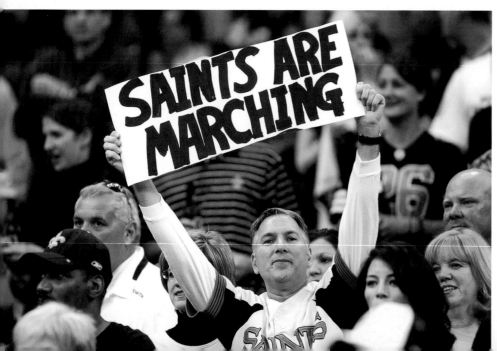

ABOVE: Fans reach for a ball tossed up by Pierre Thomas after scoring a touchdown as the New Orleans Saints defeat the Carolina Panthers 30-20 at the Superdome in New Orleans. *Leslie Westbrook/The Daily Advertiser*

RIGHT: Running back Pierre Thomas runs the ball. *Leslie Westbrook/The Daily Advertiser*

OPPOSITE LEFT: Saints running back Pierre Thomas is brought down on a run by Panthers linebacker Jon Beason.
Leslie Westbrook/The Daily Advertiser

OPPOSITE TOP RIGHT: New Orleans Saints defenders fail to bring down Carolina Panthers running back DeAngelo Williams during his run for a touchdown.
Leslie Westbrook/The Daily Advertiser

OPPOSITE BOTTOM RIGHT: Saints running back Pierre Thomas runs the ball as he is grabbed from behind by Panthers defensive tackle Hollis Thomas. *Leslie Westbrook/
The Daily Advertiser*

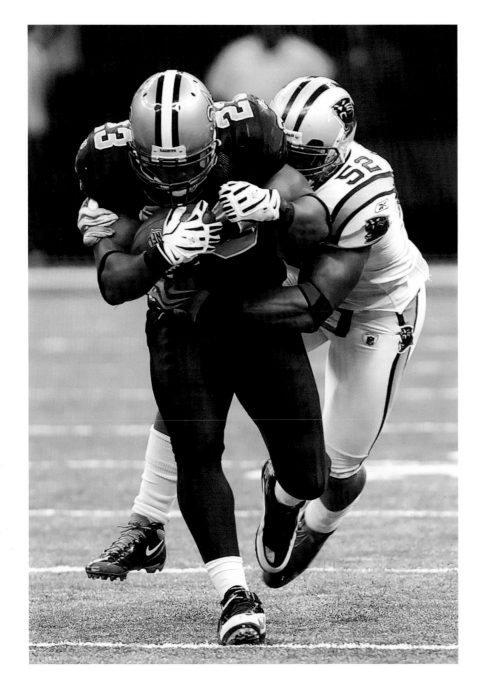

CLEANING UP

THE SECOND HALF OF THE SEASON

By Brady Aymond

With the Saints off to a franchise-best 8-0 start, the stakes — and pressure — got a little bit higher as each week of the season's second half unfolded.

Phrases like "No. 1 seed" and "16-0" started to slip out around the team's practice facility in Metairie.

The team had already established itself as a contender. Now, they wanted to take it a step further.

The first major step came on November 30 in the Louisiana Superdome as Tom Brady and the New England Patriots came to town

for a highly-anticipated game on Monday Night Football.

Two weeks removed from a 35-34 loss to the unbeaten Indianapolis Colts, the Patriots arrived in New Orleans out to prove a point.

The Saints, despite being 10-0 at the time, also seemingly needed to prove a point.

Amazingly, there were some who still had "questions" about the Saints. Surely, Brady and Bill Belichick would prove those doubters right.

Wrong.

Drew Brees abused a Belichick defense like never before, passing for 371 yards and five TDs as the Saints dismantled the Patriots, 38-17. Brees' perfect passer rating of 158.3 was a first against a Belichick defense, as

was the five touchdown passes.

Meanwhile, the Saints defense intercepted and sacked Brady twice, forcing the Patriots to declare "No mas" and pull their starters with five minutes remaining on the game clock.

"They are a real good football team, probably the best we've played all season," New England defensive lineman Vince Wilfork said.

Fate seemed to reward the Saints for their red-hot start, as the ball bounced their way in the second half of the season.

First came a miracle win at Washington, when Shaun Suisham missed a short field goal, allowing the Saints to rally in the final minute of regulation for the tying touchdown. Garrett Hartley's 18-yard field goal

won it in overtime.

Then came the unlikely stretch run, when the Saints' 24-17 loss to the Dallas Cowboys snapped their 13-game win streak and turned into a three-game losing streak to end the season.

But while the Saints were mired in a late-season slump, the rest of the NFC was following suit.

Minnesota, which went into December trailing the Saints by one game for the top seed, lost three of four to allow New Orleans to clinch the No. 1 seed prior to the season finale at Carolina.

But it was clear the Saints weren't satisfied.

"We have to play better," Saints coach Sean Payton said. "We have a lot to clean up." ✣

WEEK 10

Saints vs. Rams

W 28-23

RIGHT: New Orleans Saints players huddle together for a pre-game chant before their 24-17 loss to the Dallas Cowboys Saturday, December 19, 2009, at the Superdome.
Leslie Westbrook/The Daily Advertiser

OPPOSITE: Fans cheer the Saints on as the team defeats the Carolina Panthers 30-20 at the Superdome, November 3, 2009. *Leslie Westbrook/ The Daily Advertiser*

1B | Sports

Monday, November 16, 2009   theadvertiser.com   The Advertiser

2009 GMC Sierra Ext. Cab
$16,990
4750 JOHNSTON STREET, Lafayette
337-769-4500

BestBets

Web Extra

LSU fans had the right play called on Saturday

Beat writer **Glenn Guilbeau** says LSU fans had it right during the La. Tech game and head coach **Les Miles** had it wrong — the Tigers' play-calling should have focused on the running game and not the passing of **Jarrett Lee**.

www.theadvertiser.com

Sports in brief

Johnson wins at Phoenix to cruise into finale

AVONDALE, Ariz. — Jimmie Johnson rebounded from a rare bad race with a dominating victory at Phoenix International Raceway that pushed him to the edge of a NASCAR record fourth consecutive championship.

Johnson led 238 laps Sunday to win for the fourth time in the last five races at Phoenix. It was his seventh victory of the season, and the fourth since the start of the Chase for the Sprint Cup championship.

More important, it stretched his lead to 108 points over Hendrick Motorsports teammate Mark Martin heading into the finale at Homestead-Miami Speedway. Johnson needs to finish 25th or better next week to grab a spot in NASCAR's record books.

Although his team initially celebrated as if the title had been locked up, the No. 48 crew quickly settled down in Victory Lane.

"I can't put my guard down," Johnson said, "anything and everything can go wrong."

It did a week ago in Texas, where Johnson was caught in a wreck three laps into the race and had to sit inside his disabled race car as his crew did a total rebuild of the Chevrolet. He limped to a 38th-place finish that cost him 111 points in the standings.

Martin finished fourth, respectable but not the showing he needed to move closer to the championship that has eluded him his entire NASCAR career. The sentimental favorite this year will likely finish second in the final standings for a fifth time.

New College Rankings

Associated Press Top 10

Team	Record	Pvs
1. Florida	10-0	1
2. Alabama	10-0	2
3. Texas	10-0	2
4. TCU	10-0	4
5. Cincinnati	10-0	5
6. Boise St.	10-0	6
7. Georgia Tech	10-1	7
8. Pittsburgh	9-1	9
9. Ohio St.	9-2	10
10. LSU	8-2	9

Complete Polls = Page 2B

Only on the Web

UL Blog
Daily Advertiser writer **Joshua Parrott** keeps fans of Ragin' Cajuns athletics up to date with all things UL with his daily blog.

For these features and more, go to theadvertiser.com.

GetPublished
Share your news, photos and events

E-mail: sports@theadvertiser.com
Call: 289-6303
Fax: 371-3341
Mail: The Daily Advertiser, 1100 Bertrand Drive, Lafayette, LA 70506

SAINTS 28 ● RAMS 23

The Great Escape

Upset bid averted as Saints go to 9-0

The Associated Press

ST. LOUIS — Reggie Bush helped the New Orleans Saints overcome another bundle of mistakes to stay unbeaten for the best start in team history.

Bush scored twice for the first time in more than a year and Drew Brees compensated for two interceptions with two touchdown passes that allowed the Saints to escape with a 28-23 victory Sunday over the St. Louis Rams.

Courtney Roby opened the second half with a 97-yard kickoff return and Robert Meachem's 27-yard grab early in the fourth quarter gave New Orleans (9-0) just enough breathing room to tie the franchise record with nine straight wins.

"You're not going to blow everyone out," said cornerback Randall Gay, who played on the Patriots' 16-0 team in 2007. "It's a lot harder to blow teams out when for a lot of teams, this is like their playoff game."

Marc Bulger's 19-yard pass to Donnie Avery made it a five-point game with 2:44 to go and the Rams (1-8) made it to the New Orleans 32 before Bulger threw incomplete into the end zone on the final play.

The Rams had no timeouts on their final drive and burned a lot of clock on Bulger's 5-yard checkdown to Steven Jackson the previous play, leaving them just enough time for one final snap.

"It would have been really nice to pull it off," Bulger said. "There's a reason they're unbeaten. They made plays when they had to."

The Rams had a season high for points against a defense that played most of the second half without both starting cornerbacks. Tracy Porter limped off with a left knee injury in the opening minute and Jabari Greer was inactive because of a hurt groin.

Turnovers hurt more. The Saints had three for a four-game total of 13.

They also stalled on offense late in the game, scoring fewer than 30 points for the first time in five games, and opening the door for the Rams.

"We're not content with

See SAINTS on Page 4B

■ HISTORIC START

Sunday wasn't the picture of perfection, but the Saints are now 9-0 for the first time in the franchise's 43-year history.

■ PESKY RAMS

The near-upset mirrored a meeting in 2007 when an 0-8 Rams club shocked the Saints in the Superdome, 37-29.

St. Louis running back Steven Jackson was a monster against the Saints, rushing for 131 yards and a score, plus catching nine passes for 45 yards.

Photos by The Associated Press

New Orleans Saints defensive end Will Smith celebrates with teammate Usama Young after St. Louis Rams running back Steven Jackson was stopped on a crucial fourth-down play during the closing minutes on Sunday. In a game that ended with a pass into the end zone for the win by the Rams, the Saints survived, 28-23, on the road for the franchise's first 9-0 start.

THUMBS UP & DOWN ON SAINTS' NINTH STRAIGHT VICTORY

BREES WAS OFF
Drew Brees threw 2 INTs and passed for just 217 yards against the NFL's No. 22 pass defense.

DEFENSE STRUGGLES
With several key starters out, the Saints' defense gave up 434 yards to the Rams' 26th-ranked offense.

ROBY'S RETURN KEY
Courtney Roby's kickoff return for a TD to start the second half was the first since 2004 for the Saints.

WEEK 10 SCOREBOARD

Tennessee	41	Miami	25	Cincinnati	18	Minnesota	27	Green Bay	31	Arizona	31
Buffalo	17	Tampa Bay	23	Pittsburgh	12	Detroit	10	Dallas	7	Seattle	20
Washington	27	Jacksonville	24	Carolina	28	Kansas City	16	San Diego	31	Indianapolis	35
Denver	17	N.Y. Jets	22	Atlanta	19	Oakland	10	Philadelphia	23	New England	34

UL's dream of a late run ended at MTSU

MURFREESBORO, Tenn. — Starting to think that UL is cursed after watching the injuries continue to pile up in a 34-17 loss to Middle Tennessee on Saturday at Floyd Stadium. Here are some questions, concerns and observations after the road loss.

Q&A

Any dreams that the Ragin' Cajuns (5-5, 3-3 Sun Belt) had of making a late run to earn a share of the Sun Belt Conference title disappeared Saturday as quickly as their offense and defense in the second half.

The no-show in the final 30 minutes was a huge letdown after UL's most complete performance of the season the previous week in a win at Arkansas State.

Unless the Cajuns can win the next two games against UL Monroe and Troy at home to hit the seven-win mark, their bowl drought will be extended to 39 years.

The most likely scenario is UL wins one of its two final two games to reach the six-win mark for the fourth time in five years.

See CAJUNS on Page 4B

Joshua Parrott
jparrott@theadvertiser.com

Williams fills void in backfield for Tigers

Glenn Guilbeau
gguilbeau@gannett.com

LSU TIGERS FOOTBALL

BATON ROUGE — When Charles Scott didn't get up following his 34-yard run at Alabama two weeks ago, his buddy and backup, Keiland Williams, thought he just got the wind knocked out of him.

"So I was going to run out there and mess with him. When I got there, I saw his eyes, and he was holding his shoulder," Williams said Saturday night after LSU defeated Louisiana Tech, 24-16. "I just grabbed his hand and let him know I was there for him."

Scott, a senior from Saline, will likely not play for LSU again because he broke his collarbone on that play Williams, a senior from Lafayette, may be LSU's featured back for

See TIGERS on Page 2B

FOR HOME DELIVERY, CALL 800-259-8852

BestBets

Web Extra

Did Les Miles try to avoid blame after Ole Miss loss?

Readers can find the transcript from LSU coach **Les Miles'** press conference after the loss at Ole Miss and draw their own conclusions as to whether Miles tried to push blame onto others for the mismanaged final seconds.

www.theadvertiser.com

Sports in brief

Johnson wraps up record 4th straight series title

HOMESTEAD, Fla. — **Jimmie Johnson** is a NASCAR record fourth consecutive championship with a fifth-place finish in the Sprint Cup series finale at Homestead-Miami Speedway on Sunday.

Johnson needed only to finish 25th or better to beat teammate **Mark Martin** in the race, won by **Denny Hamlin**, to give team owner **Rick Hendrick** his own NASCAR record, a 12th championship.

"History, boys!" Johnson shouted as he crossed the finish line. "How about some history?"

The day also cemented Hendrick Motorsports as the dominant Sprint Cup racing team. Martin wound up with the fifth runner-up finish of his career in the final standings, while **Jeff Gordon** was third.

"I feel really, really blessed to have had a chance," Martin said. Upon leaving his car in Victory Lane, Johnson thanked the fans, tears sparkling in his eyes.

"Man, it's going to take a while to sink in," he said.

He joins **Richard Petty** (7), **Dale Earnhardt** (7) and teammate **Jeff Gordon** (4) as the only drivers to win more than three titles.

"To do something that's never been done in the sport, and love the sport like I do and respect it like I do and the greats — Petty, Earnhardt, Gordon — to do something they have never done is so awesome," Johnson said. "And to win four championships in eight years, what this team has done — this is unbelievable."

Johnson's won 47 races since 2002 and never finished lower than fifth in the final standings.

New College Rankings

Associated Press Top 10

Team	Record	Pvs
1. Florida	11-0	1
2. Alabama	11-0	2
3. Texas	11-0	3
4. TCU	11-0	4
5. Cincinnati	10-0	5
6. Boise St.	11-0	6
7. Georgia Tech	10-1	7
8. Pittsburgh	9-1	8
9. Ohio St.	10-2	9
10. Oregon	9-2	11

Complete Polls on Page 2B

Only on the Web

UL Blog
Daily Advertiser writer Joshua Parrott keeps fans of Ragin' Cajuns athletics up to date with all things UL with his daily blog.

For these features and more, go to theadvertiser.com.

GetPublished
Share your news, photos and events

E-mail: sports@theadvertiser.com
Call: 289-6303
Fax: 371-3341
Mail: The Daily Advertiser 1100 Bertrand Drive Lafayette, LA 70506

SAINTS 38 • BUCS 7

Saints a Perfect 10

Photos by The Associated Press

Robert Meachem continued to play a big role in the passing game with two short touchdown catches in the runaway win at Tampa Bay.

Winning streak a new record for franchise

■ **PATRIOTS ARE NEXT**
Start counting the days. Next Monday, the Saints host New England. The Patriots are the last team to venture through a season undefeated in 2007.

■ **BUCS OVERMATCHED**
Led by a rookie quarterback, Tampa Bay managed just 219 yards of offense and had four turnovers against the Saints.

The Associated Press

TAMPA, Fla. — Perfect through 10 games, the New Orleans Saints think they can play even better.

"I feel like we haven't peaked yet. ... I feel like the sky's the limit for this team," Drew Brees said after throwing for three touchdowns in Sunday's 38-7 rout of the struggling Tampa Bay Buccaneers.

"It only gets harder. By no means can we sit back on what we've accomplished thus far. Every team we face would love to give us that first loss."

The Saints (10-0) shrugged off a slow start defensively, shutting down the Bucs after yielding a long touchdown drive to open the game. Offensively, they took advantage of numerous mistakes by young Tampa Bay quarterback Josh Freeman.

Robert Meachem caught touchdown passes of 4 and 6 yards in the first half, while Mike Bell scored on runs of 3 and 1 yards in the second, when New Orleans gained 147 of its 183 yards rushing.

The Saints' 10-game winning streak is the longest in franchise history.

"I like where we're at. We're 10-0 and we beat a division opponent on the road," coach Sean Payton said. "I thought we got better today."

A spate of turnovers made the Saints seem more vulnerable over the past month, but Brees didn't throw an interception for the first time in five games. The Saints also didn't allow a sack for the first time since Oct. 18 against the Giants.

Brees said the NFL's No. 1 offense can become even more efficient.

"The last four games, we kind of got back to some old habits that we didn't want to, which was the turnovers and negative plays," the quarterback said. "We needed a game like this, to come out and look sharp in all phases."

Tampa Bay (1-9) drove 95 yards for a touchdown on its first possession. But

See SAINTS on Page 4B

New Orleans Saints safety Darren Sharper (42) grabs Tampa Bay's Earnest Graham by the facemask during action in Sunday's game. Sharper was penalized on the play, but that was one of the team's few faults in a 38-7 win that improved the Saints to 10-0.

IT WAS ALL THUMBS UP FOR SAINTS IN RUNAWAY WIN

TAKEAWAY KINGS
Three more interceptions on Sunday pushed the Saints' season total to a league-leading 20.

EQUAL OPPORTUNITY
Drew Brees spread the ball to eight different receivers. Robert Meachem delivered with a pair of TD catches.

IN THE ZONE
The Saints were perfect in the red zone, scoring TDs on all five possessions inside the Tampa Bay 20.

WEEK 11 SCOREBOARD

Cleveland	37	Dallas	7	Indianapolis	35	Minnesota	36	New England	31
Detroit	38	Washington	6	Baltimore	17	Seattle	9	N.Y. Jets	14
N.Y. Giants	34	Green Bay	30	Kansas City	27	Arizona	21	San Diego	32
Atlanta	31	San Francisco	24	Pittsburgh	24	St. Louis	13	Denver	3

(New Orleans 38 Tampa Bay 7 / Jacksonville 24 Buffalo 15 / Oakland 20 Cincinnati 17 / Philadelphia 24 Chicago 20)

LSU coaches remake 'Dumb and Dumber'

Glenn Guilbeau
gguilbeau@gannett.com

BATON ROUGE — LSU coach Les Miles closed practices before this season. So the question is, is the team practicing? And exactly what is that offense practicing?

Let's be honest, LSU's offense looks like the most poorly drilled unit in the nation. After Saturday's debacle in Oxford, Miss., in which LSU's offensive

coaches on the sideline and in the pressbox blew a chance to try a game-winning field goal against Ole Miss, the world knows what those objective and close to this team have known for years. LSU's sideline is a chaotic joke.

No one knows this better than quarterback Jordan Jefferson. Three times after

Saturday's 25-23 loss, Jefferson used the word "confusion" when discussing his team's sideline. Quarterbacks tend to look to their sideline for guidance. When Jefferson looks over there, he gets more and more misguided.

See GUILBEAU on Page 2B

McGuire, Green keys to huge win over ULM

Joshua Parrott
parrott@theadvertiser.com

UL FOOTBALL REWIND

Wondering where the UL team that showed up Saturday came from and beat UL Monroe, 21-17, on Saturday at Cajun Field has been for the past month. Here are some other thoughts and observations from the win amid rainy conditions.

Anyone wondering exactly how much the Ragin' Cajuns (6-5, 4-3 Sun Belt) had missed canceled

back Brad McGuire and tight end Ladarius Green over the past three games got a definitive answer Saturday.

McGuire, a run-first quarterback, ran seven times for only 11 yards, but had a pair of rushing touchdowns and three fourth-down conversions. The sophomore had been

See CAJUNS on Page 4B

FOR HOME DELIVERY, CALL 800-259-8852

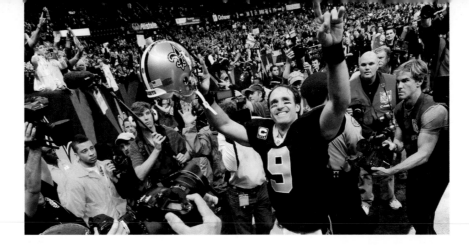

NOVEMBER 30, 2009

WEEK 12

**Saints
vs. Patriots**

W 38-17

RIGHT: Saints wide receiver Devery Henderson runs for a touchdown after catching a pass in the second quarter against the Patriots Monday, Nov. 29, 2009, at the Superdome in New Orleans. *Denny Culbert/The Daily Advertiser*

PREVIOUS TOP LEFT: New Orleans quarterback Drew Brees smiles up at the Saints faithful as he exits the field after defeating the Patriots. The Saints won 38-17. *Denny Culbert/The Daily Advertiser*

PREVIOUS BOTTOM LEFT: Saints fans hope to be 11-0 after the game against the New England Patriots. They were granted their wish. *Denny Culbert/The Daily Advertiser*

PREVIOUS RIGHT: The Saints' Will Smith takes the field before the game. *Denny Culbert/The Daily Advertiser*

ABOVE: The Saints defense stops running back Laurence Maroney. *Denny Culbert/The Daily Advertiser*

TOP LEFT: The Saints' Robert Meachem scores a touchdown against the Patriots.
Denny Culbert/The Daily Advertiser

LEFT: Jonathan Goodwin celebrates during the win over the Patriots.
Denny Culbert/The Daily Advertiser

LEFT: The Saints' Mike McKenzie avoids the grasp of Randy Moss. McKenzie was inactive at the end of the season, but was a key factor in the Patriots game. *Denny Culbert/ The Daily Advertiser*

BOTTOM LEFT: Darren Sharper gains yards for the Saints. *Denny Culbert/ The Daily Advertiser*

OPPOSITE: The Saints' David Thomas fights off Brandon Meriweather at the Super-dome in New Orleans. *Denny Culbert/ The Daily Advertiser*

BELOW: Saints running back Pierre Thomas celebrates with teammates Jermon Bushrod, left, and David Thomas after scoring a touchdown, in the second quarter. *Denny Culbert/The Daily Advertiser*

DECEMBER 6, 2009

WEEK 13

Saints
vs. Redskins

W 33-30

1B | Sports

Monday, December 7, 2009   theadvertiser.com   The Advertiser

BestBets

NFL Inside

Saints get breathing room as Vikings lose at Arizona

There was no magic for Brett Favre and the Minnesota Vikings on Sunday night during a 30-17 loss at Arizona. The loss was the Vikings' second and a boost for the New Orleans Saints attaining the NFC's top seed and home-field advantage for the playoffs.

NFL Blitz • Page 3B

Sports in brief

Manning, Colts keep piling up the records

INDIANAPOLIS — Peyton **Manning** keeps finding new winning formulas, and the Colts keep making history.

Instead of another patented comeback or impressive air show, Manning opened December by playing keepaway from Tennessee and leading the Colts to a 27-17 victory for their record-tying 21st consecutive regular-season win.

Manning

"You try to tell these guys that when you win a couple in a row, or three or four in a row, this is not normal," the three-time MVP said. "It's not normal to win 10 or 11 or 12 games every year."

For Indy (12-0), the milestones all seem commonplace.

Sunday's list included:
■ Matching New England's record, set from 2006-08, with a chance to break it next week at home against Denver.
■ Extending their own NFL record of consecutive 12-win seasons to seven.
■ Remaining undefeated, the first time in league history two teams — New Orleans is also 12-0 — have been unbeaten this late in the season.
■ And tying the 1990s San Francisco 49ers for most wins in a decade (113).

"It (the record) is one of those things we talk about. We kind of identify the milestones on Wednesday morning when we get in. We talk about some of the things we're accomplishing," coach Jim Caldwell said. "The guys appreciate it, but it's not something that goes to their heads."

New College Rankings

Associated Press Top 10

Team	Record	Pvs
1. Alabama	13-0	2
2. Texas	13-0	3
3. TCU	12-0	4
4. Cincinnati	12-0	5
5. Florida	12-1	1
6. Boise St.	13-0	6
7. Oregon	10-2	7
8. Ohio St.	10-2	8
9. Georgia Tech	11-2	12
10. Iowa	10-2	9

Complete Polls • Page 2B

Only on the Web

UL Blog
Daily Advertiser writer **Joshua Parrott** keeps fans of Ragin' Cajuns athletics up to date with all things UL with his daily blog.

For these features and more, go to **theadvertiser.com.**

GetPublished

Share your news, photos and events

E-mail: sports@theadvertiser.com
Call: 289-6303
Fax: 371-3341
Mail: The Daily Advertiser
1100 Bertrand Drive
Lafayette, LA 70506

SAINTS 33 • REDSKINS 30

PERFECT ENDING

Dramatic OT victory moves Saints to 12-0

■ IS IT DESTINY?
Robert Meachem scored on a zany fumble return following an INT by Washington and the 'Skins missed a late 23-yard FG that would have put N.O. away.

■ CLINCH THE SOUTH
The Saints already had clinched the NFC South title, following Philadelphia's win at Atlanta, prior to the dramatic finish.

Photos by The Associated Press

Saints defensive back Chris McAlister (29) comes from behind to recover a fumble by Washington's Mike Sellers that set up the winning field goal in OT.

Running back Mike Bell climbed into the stands and celebrated with fans of the New Orleans Saints following the team's improbable late comeback that led to a 33-30 overtime win over the Washington Redskins at FedEx Field in Landover, Md.

The Associated Press

LANDOVER, Md. — The New Orleans Saints had no business winning. Two of their biggest plays were unbelievable flukes, bad mistakes that somehow morphed into positive results. Then they needed the other team's kicker to miss a 23-yard field goal just to stay alive, and a freeze-frame replay reversal to get the ball in overtime.

But the Saints are living a charmed life these days, and the Washington Redskins are as snakebit as can be. New Orleans trailed by 10 in the fourth quarter Sunday and played more than four quarters without holding a lead — until Garrett Hartley kicked an 18-yard field goal 6:29 into the extra period for a 33-30 win.

"I don't know about the voodoo, but I definitely believe in destiny," said Drew Brees, who led a no-timeout, 80-yard drive in just 33 seconds to tie the game late in regulation. "I believe in karma, and what goes around comes around. We've been on the other side of this deal probably too many times, and maybe it's our time, that we start catching some of the breaks."

Catching those breaks? That sure explains how the Saints are now 12-0 with the NFC South title in hand. How else to explain a badly shanked punt that turns into a 29-yard gain, or an interception by Brees that somehow becomes a touchdown for teammate Robert Meachem?

"Crazy plays," linebacker Jonathan Vilma said. "When you're hot, you're hot. And sometimes it's better to be lucky than good."

New Orleans also showed it can brave the cold, winning a sub-40 degree game for the first time since 1995. Well, maybe. The defense, led by former Redskins defensive coordinator Gregg Williams, offered minimal resistance, allowing Washington to pile up 455

See SAINTS on Page 2B

THUMBS UP & DOWN ON SAINTS' NARROW WIN IN D.C.

IT'S BEEN AWHILE
The victory was the first for the Saints in OT since beating Atlanta, 23-20, at home on Nov. 16, 2003.

SOFT SECONDARY
After holding Tom Brady to 237 yards and no TDs, Jason Campbell ripped N.O. for 367 yards and 3 scores.

M*A*S*H UNIT
The Saints found a way to win with LB Scott Fujita and CBs Randall Gay and Jabari Greer inactive.

WEEK 13 SCOREBOARD

Chicago	17	Denver	44	Cincinnati	23	New Orleans	33	San Diego	16	Seattle	30
St. Louis	9	Kansas City	24	Detroit	6	Washington	13	Tampa Bay	30	San Francisco	20
Oakland	27	Philadelphia	34	Miami	22	Indianapolis	27	Jacksonville	23	Arizona	31
Pittsburgh	24	Atlanta	7	New England	21	Tennessee	17	Houston	18	Dallas	6	N.Y. Giants	24	Minnesota	30

Bowl season is Miles' favorite time of year

BATON ROUGE — Les Miles is back in his comfort zone. It's beginning to look a lot like bowl season, and this is Miles' time of year.

Give him two weeks off and two weeks of practice, and he'll ruin an opponent's New Year's.

Les Miles is not a minute man. Check the Ole Miss game for that and a few others.

Les Miles is a month man. Check his bowl scoreboard. It's Miles 57, Opponents 44. That's an average final score of 39-11.

And he doesn't care what type of team he plays. Three times he has defeated higher-ranked teams. He has beaten the sacred cows — Notre Dame and Ohio State. He beat the bad boys — Miami. He

best old school Georgia Tech and its triple option. Tech was No. 14, and LSU was not even ranked in that game. And he has beaten them all badly.

He beat two coaches who later got fired — Miami's Larry Coker and Notre Dame's

See BOWL on Page 4B

It's Miles vs. JoePa in Capital One Bowl

Glenn Guilbeau
gguilbeau@gannett.com

BATON ROUGE — LSU is off to Disney World to play against a coach older than Mickey Mouse.

The No. 13 Tigers (9-3) will play No. 11 Penn State (10-2) in the Capital One Bowl on Jan. 1 in Orlando, Fla., at noon on ABC. The Nittany Lions are coached by 82-year-old Joe Paterno, the winningest Division I-A college football coach in

history with 393 victories.

Mickey Mouse, the face of the Walt Disney Company for decades, was created by the late Walt Disney in 1928. Paterno, who was born on Dec. 21, 1926, will be 83 by game time.

"I don't know that I've ever not been aware of Joe Paterno," LSU coach Les Miles, 56, said shortly after accepting the invitation from the Capital One

See LSU on Page 4B

The newspaper clipping

1B | **Sports**

Monday, December 14, 2009 · theadvertiser.com · The Advertiser

BestBets

NFL Inside

Colts set record with 22nd straight victory

Tight end **Dallas Clark** had three TD receptions as Indianapolis beat Denver, 28-16, to shatter NFL records for consecutive wins in the regular season (22) and most wins in a decade (114), plus wrapping up home-field advantage for the playoffs.

Story → Page 4B

Sports in brief

Denver WR Marshall sets record with 21 catches

INDIANAPOLIS — Brandon Marshall didn't enjoy his single-game receptions record much.

That's because his 21 grabs came in Denver's 28-16 loss to Indianapolis on Sunday.

"I believe it was one of those games where, whenever you accomplish something like that, it definitely feels good," he said. "But we have goals, and our only goal is to win games. I'd definitely trade in a couple of those catches for a win."

Marshall surpassed the mark San Francisco's **Terrell Owens** set on Dec. 17, 2000. He finished with 200 yards and two touchdowns and bettered his team record of 18 catches, set on Sept. 14, 2008, against San Diego.

He tied Owens' mark on a 5-yard touchdown pass from **Kyle Orton** in the fourth quarter. He set the record on Denver's final offensive play when he gained 7 yards on a fourth-down play before lateraling to lineman **Chris Kuper** for 7 more yards.

Marshall had 10 catches at halftime and 15 at the end of the third quarter. He was told he was nearing the record.

"Someone came up to me and said I was close, but I didn't have an idea of where I was," he said. Orton completed 29 of 41 passes for 277 yards. He targeted Marshall 28 times, despite heavy coverage.

College Football

Kansas hires Turner Gill as head football coach

LAWRENCE, Kan. — Kansas has hired former Nebraska quarterback and assistant coach **Turner Gill** as its new head football coach.

The university officially announced the offer Saturday.

The Associated Press had reported Saturday evening that the 47-year-old had accepted the offer of a multiyear contract to replace **Mark Mangino.**

Gill has been head coach at Buffalo the past four years and took the Bulls to the Mid-American Conference title in 2008. He will be introduced at a news conference today.

Only on the Web

UL Blog

Daily Advertiser writer **Joshua Parrott** keeps fans of Ragin' Cajuns athletics up to date with all things UL with his daily blog.

For these features and more, go to theadvertiser.com.

GetPublished

Share your news, photos and events

E-mail: sports@theadvertiser.com
Call: 289-6303
Fax: 371-3341
Mail: The Daily Advertiser 1100 Bertrand Drive Lafayette, LA 70506

SAINTS 26 • FALCONS 23

Lucky No. 13

RECORD SHATTERED
The Saints' magical march now includes the most wins in a season in club history.

GUARANTEED BYE
By virtue of Sunday's win, the Saints earned a crucial first-round bye in playoffs.

New Orleans Saints linebacker Jonathan Vilma celebrates after stopping the Atlanta Falcons on fourth down in the final seconds of the fourth quarter to preserve a 26-23 road win in the NFC South on Sunday at the Georgia Dome. The victory moved the undefeated Saints to 13-0, set a franchise record for wins in a season and secured a bye in the first round of the playoffs. — The Associated Press

Saints dodge another minefield as perfect season stays intact

The Associated Press

ATLANTA — The New Orleans Saints are still perfect, which is all that matters.

They're not the least bit worried about another close call.

Drew Brees threw for 296 yards and three touchdowns, Jonathan Vilma came up with two huge defensive plays, and the Saints pulled out another tight win, 26-23, over the pesky Atlanta Falcons on Sunday.

A week ago, New Orleans (13-0) appeared on the verge of losing until Washington missed a chip-shot field goal in regulation. The Saints rallied for a 33-30 overtime win.

This time, they struggled to hold off an Atlanta team that was missing injured stars Matt Ryan and Michael Turner. The result was in doubt until Vilma came up with a crushing fourth-down hit on Jason Snelling, stopping him a yard short of the marker with just over a minute remaining.

New Orleans joined Indianapolis, also a winner Sunday, as one of seven teams to reach 13-0 in NFL history. Still these last two games have been the closest margins of a season dominated by double-digit wins.

A cause for concern?

"Why would we be concerned? We're 13-0," Vilma said. "You're not going to get many blowout wins in the NFL."

Or, as Brees said, "We call that being battle-tested."

While lacking in style points, New Orleans set a franchise record for wins in a season, clinched a first-round bye in the playoffs and moved a step closer to home-field advantage throughout the NFC playoffs.

"It's only going to get harder from here on out," Brees said. But "no matter what the situation, we always feel like we have an opportunity to win. Whether it's our

See SAINTS on Page 4B

Did You Know?

BEST STARTS IN HISTORY

Here's a look at the only teams in NFL history to start a season 13-0 and where the streak ended:

2007	New England	16-0
1972	Miami Dolphins	14-0
1934	Chicago	13-0
1998	Denver Broncos	13-0
2005	Indianapolis Colts	13-0
2009	**New Orleans**	**13-0**
2009	Indianapolis	13-0

See UL on Page 2B

THUMBS UP & DOWN ON SAINTS' 13TH STRAIGHT WIN

REGGIE A FACTOR
Reggie Bush averaged more than six yards on 12 touches in the game and scored a pair of TDs.

SECONDARY ISSUES
In just his 12th career start, backup QB Chris Redman riddled the Saints for 303 yards passing and 1 TD.

BREES ON RISE
QB Drew Brees threw three TD passes for 200 in his career, which ranks 30th in NFL history.

2009 GMC Sierra 1500 Crew Cab

$10,000 off
4750 JOHNSTON STREET, LAFAYETTE
337-769-4500

Joshua Parrott

Johnson has helped right Cajuns' ship

Soon after speaking with the media following an eight-point loss at LSU on Dec. 1, UL forward Tyren Johnson made a simple request as he walked back to the team's locker room.

"Don't give up on us yet," Johnson said to one particular reporter. "We're going to turn things around."

The Ragin' Cajuns (3-4, 1-0 Sun Belt) appear to have turned things around with back-to-back wins, and the versatile Johnson has led that charge with a pair of Herculean efforts.

Four days after losing at LSU, Johnson fell just short of the program's first triple-double in four years with 11 points, 14 rebounds and seven assists in a 90-85 win over Sam Houston State. FOXSports.com's Jeff Goodman honored Johnson, who made 13-of-17 shots in the win, as his Mid-Major Stud of the Day.

Johnson followed with 23 points, nine rebounds, three assists and two blocked shots in an 81-74 win over Florida Atlantic on Saturday as UL won its Sun Belt Conference opener for the third straight season.

The 6-foot-8 senior is still committing too many turnovers (34 in seven games), but his mistakes will decrease as he adjusts to becoming more involved as a playmaker.

His leadership, whether leading by example or the occasional word now and then, has given the Cajuns some much-needed momentum going into Tuesday's game at Southern Miss.

Johnson has also made himself an early contender for Sun Belt Player of the Year honors along with Troy guard Brandon Hazzard, Denver guard/forward Nate Rohnert and Western Kentucky guard A.J. Slaughter. He is currently the only player to rank among

Tyren Johnson has scored 54 points and added 23 boards in the Cajuns' last two games. — Daily Advertiser file photo

---

WEEK 14 SCOREBOARD

Houston	34	Baltimore	48	Buffalo	16	New England	20	Miami 14
Seattle	7	Detroit	3	Kansas City	10	Carolina	10	Jacksonville 10
Green Bay	21	New Orleans	26	Indianapolis	28	N.Y. Jets	26	Minnesota 30
Chicago	14	Atlanta	23	Denver	16	Tampa Bay	3	Cincinnati 10

Tennessee	47	San Diego	20
St. Louis	7	Dallas	17
Washington	34	Philadelphia	45
Oakland	13	N.Y. Giants	38

FOR HOME DELIVERY, CALL 800-259-8852

The scrapbook overlay

DECEMBER 13, 2009

WEEK 14

Saints vs. Falcons

W 26-23

ABOVE: Saints fans cheer their team to a 48-27 win over the Giants on Sunday, Oct. 18, 2009, at the Superdome. *Denny Culbert/The Daily Advertiser*

OPPOSITE: Fans hold up signs during the New Orleans Saints' 24-17 loss to the Dallas Cowboys Saturday, December 19, 2009, at the Superdome. *Leslie Westbrook/The Daily Advertiser*

WEEK 15

**Saints
vs. Cowboys**

L 24-17

ABOVE: A pass falls incomplete as Cowboys wide receiver Roy Williams is hit from behind by Saints cornerback Tracy Porter during the New Orleans Saints' 24-17 loss to the Dallas Cowboys.
Leslie Westbrook/The Daily Advertiser

LEFT: Saints head coach Sean Payton argues with an official.
Leslie Westbrook/The Daily Advertiser

OPPOSITE LEFT: A Saints fan watches the final moments tick away.
Leslie Westbrook/The Daily Advertiser

OPPOSITE RIGHT: Saints quarterback Drew Brees looks to pass.
Leslie Westbrook/The Daily Advertiser

RIGHT: Saints tight end David Thomas runs with the ball. *Leslie Westbrook/The Daily Advertiser*

OPPOSITE LEFT: Saints running back Pierre Thomas is locked up during a run by Cowboys defensive end Igor Olshansky. *Leslie Westbrook/The Daily Advertiser*

OPPOSITE TOP RIGHT: Saints wide receiver Robert Meachem is brought down by Cowboys cornerback Orlando Scandrick. *Leslie Westbrook/The Daily Advertiser*

OPPOSITE MIDDLE RIGHT: Cowboys running back Marion Barber slips past Saints cornerback Malcolm Jenkins. *Leslie Westbrook/ The Daily Advertiser*

OPPOSITE BOTTOM RIGHT: Saints quarterback Drew Brees congratulates Cowboys quarterback Tony Romo after the New Orleans Saints' 24-17 loss. *Leslie Westbrook/ The Daily Advertiser*

DECEMBER 27, 2009

WEEK 16

**Saints
vs. Buccaneers**

L 20-17

ABOVE: New Orleans linebacker Anthony Waters tries to pump up the crowd before the overtime kickoff to Tampa Bay. The Saints lost 20-17 in overtime to the Buccaneers. *Denny Culbert/The Daily Advertiser*

LEFT: Saints running back Reggie Bush pushes away Tampa Bay cornerback Ronde Barber to gain a few more rushing yards in the first quarter. *Denny Culbert/The Daily Advertiser*

OPPOSITE LEFT: Running back Reggie Bush narrowly avoids Bucs linebacker Geno Hayes. *Denny Culbert/The Daily Advertiser*

OPPOSITE RIGHT: New Orleans coach Sean Payton argues with an official after a call in the second half. *Denny Culbert/ The Daily Advertiser*

TOP RIGHT: The Saints' Darren Sharper, left, and Malcolm Jenkins attempt to stop Tampa Bay's Kellen Winslow. *Denny Culbert/ The Daily Advertiser*

BOTTOM LEFT: Saints quarterback Drew Brees. *Denny Culbert/The Daily Advertiser*

BOTTOM RIGHT: A Saints fan expresses his feelings by tearing his sign and yelling insults as the team left the field. *Denny Culbert/ The Daily Advertiser*

OPPOSITE: Saints fans Monica Quintana, from St. Martinville, looks on as her team leaves the field after losing in overtime to the Tampa Bay at the Superdome. The Saints lost 20-17 in overtime to the Buccaneers. *Denny Culbert/The Daily Advertiser*

PREVIOUS TOP LEFT: Tampa Bay cornerback Ronde Barber and New Orleans wide receiver Marques Colston race to recover a fumble by Colston. Tampa recovered the football. *Denny Culbert/The Daily Advertiser*

PREVIOUS BOTTOM LEFT: New Orleans running back Pierre Thomas trots into the endzone for the first touchdown of the game. *Denny Culbert/The Daily Advertiser*

PREVIOUS MIDDLE: The Saints' Reggie Bush looks for an opening. *Denny Culbert/ The Daily Advertiser*

PREVIOUS RIGHT: New Orleans safety Darren Sharper dives over Tampa Bay guard Davin Joseph after intercepting a pass in the first half. *Denny Culbert/The Daily Advertiser*

JANUARY 3, 2010

WEEK 17

Saints vs. Panthers

L 23-10

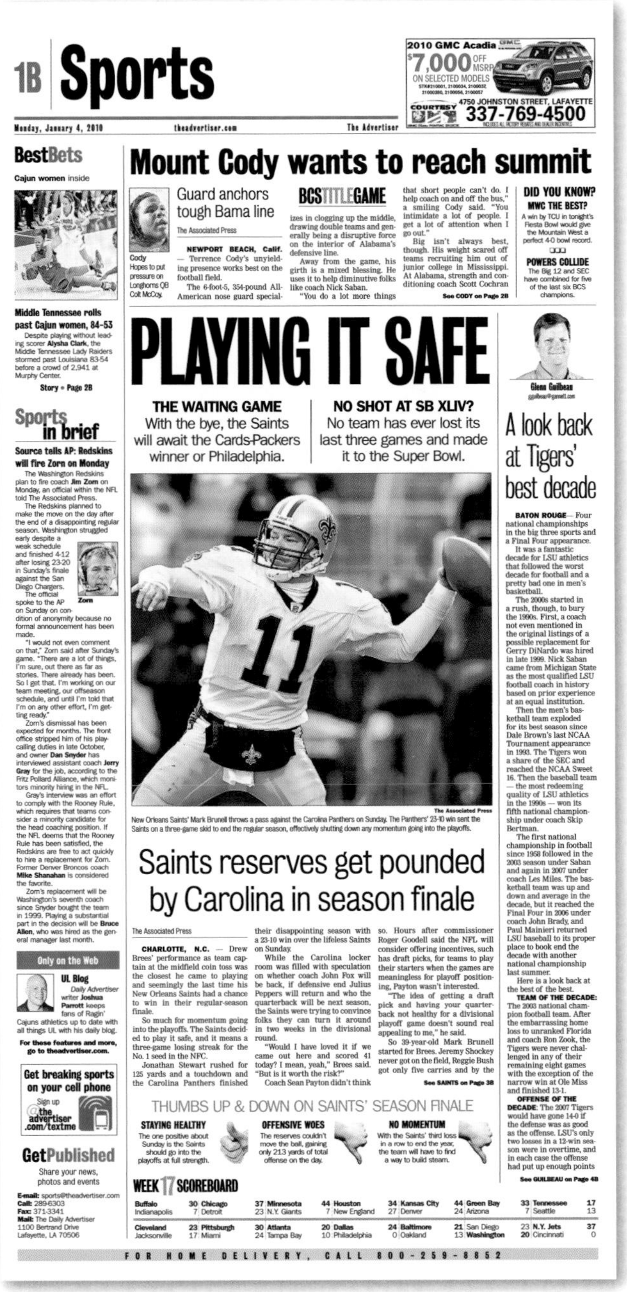

1B **Sports**

2010 GMC Acadia $7,000 OFF MSRP ON SELECTED MODELS STK#210001, 2100034, 2100037, 21000380, 2100056, 2100057 4750 JOHNSTON STREET, LAFAYETTE COURTESY 337-769-4500

Monday, January 4, 2010 theadvertiser.com The Advertiser

BestBets

Cajun women inside

Middle Tennessee rolls past Cajun women, 84-53

Despite playing without leading scorer **Alysha Clark**, the Middle Tennessee Lady Raiders stormed past Louisiana 83-54 before a crowd of 2,941 at Murphy Center.

Story • Page 2B

Mount Cody wants to reach summit

Guard anchors tough Bama line

BCS TITLE GAME

The Associated Press

Cody
Hopes to put pressure on Longhorns QB Colt McCoy.

NEWPORT BEACH, Calif. — Terrence Cody's unyielding presence works best on the football field.

The 6-foot-5, 354-pound All-American nose guard specializes in clogging up the middle, drawing double teams and generally being a disruptive force on the interior of Alabama's defensive line.

Away from the game, his girth is a mixed blessing. He uses it to help diminutive folks like coach Nick Saban.

"You do a lot more things that short people can't do. I help coach on and off the bus," a smiling Cody said. "You intimidate a lot of people. I get a lot of attention when I go out."

Big isn't always best, though. His weight scared off teams recruiting him out of junior college in Mississippi. At Alabama, strength and conditioning coach Scott Cochran

See CODY on Page 2B

DID YOU KNOW?

MWC THE BEST?
A win by TCU in tonight's Fiesta Bowl would give the Mountain West a perfect 4-0 bowl record.

POWERS COLLIDE
The Big 12 and SEC have combined for five of the last six BCS champions.

PLAYING IT SAFE

THE WAITING GAME
With the bye, the Saints will await the Cards-Packers winner or Philadelphia.

NO SHOT AT SB XLIV?
No team has ever lost its last three games and made it to the Super Bowl.

The Associated Press

New Orleans Saints' Mark Brunell throws a pass against the Carolina Panthers on Sunday. The Panthers' 23-10 win sent the Saints on a three-game skid to end the regular season, effectively shutting down any momentum going into the playoffs.

Saints reserves get pounded by Carolina in season finale

The Associated Press

CHARLOTTE, N.C. — Drew Brees' performance as team captain at the midfield coin toss was the closest he came to playing and seemingly the last time his New Orleans Saints had a chance to win in their regular-season finale.

So much for momentum going into the playoffs. The Saints decided to play it safe, and it means a three-game losing streak for the No. 1 seed in the NFC.

Jonathan Stewart rushed for 125 yards and a touchdown and the Carolina Panthers finished their disappointing season with a 23-10 win over the lifeless Saints on Sunday.

While the Carolina locker room was filled with speculation on whether coach John Fox will be back, if defensive end Julius Peppers will return and who the quarterback will be next season, the Saints were trying to convince folks they can turn it around in two weeks in the divisional round.

"Would I have loved it if we came out here and scored 41 today? I mean, yeah," Brees said. "But is it worth the risk?"

Coach Sean Payton didn't think so. Hours after commissioner Roger Goodell said the NFL will consider offering incentives, such has draft picks, for teams to play their starters when the games are meaningless for playoff positioning, Payton wasn't interested.

"The idea of getting a draft pick and having your quarterback not healthy for a divisional playoff game doesn't sound real appealing to me," he said.

So 39-year-old Mark Brunell started for Brees. Jeremy Shockey never got on the field, Reggie Bush got only five carries and by the

See SAINTS on Page 3B

THUMBS UP & DOWN ON SAINTS' SEASON FINALE

STAYING HEALTHY
The one positive about Sunday is the Saints should go into the playoffs at full strength.

OFFENSIVE WOES
The reserves couldn't move the ball, gaining only 213 yards of total offense on the day.

NO MOMENTUM
With the Saints' third loss in a row to end the year, the team will have to find a way to build steam.

Glenn Guilbeau
gguilbeau@gannett.com

A look back at Tigers' best decade

BATON ROUGE — Four national championships in the big three sports and a Final Four appearance.

It was a fantastic decade for LSU athletics that followed the worst decade for football and a pretty bad one in men's basketball.

The 2000s started in a rush, though, to bury the 1990s. First, a coach not even mentioned in the original listings of a possible replacement for Gerry DiNardo was hired in late 1999. Nick Saban came from Michigan State as the most qualified LSU football coach in history based on prior experience at an equal institution.

Then the men's basketball team exploded for its best season since Dale Brown's last NCAA Tournament appearance in 1993. The Tigers won a share of the SEC and reached the NCAA Sweet 16. Then the baseball team — the most redeeming quality of LSU athletics in the 1990s — won its fifth national championship under coach Skip Bertman.

The first national championship in football since 1958 followed in the 2003 season under Saban and again in 2007 under coach Les Miles. The basketball team was up and down and average in the decade, but it reached the Final Four in 2006 under coach John Brady, and Paul Mainieri returned LSU baseball to its proper place to book end the decade with another national championship last summer.

Here is a look back at the best of the best.

TEAM OF THE DECADE: The 2003 national champion football team. After the embarrassing home loss to unranked Florida and coach Ron Zook, the Tigers were never challenged in any of their remaining eight games with the exception of the narrow win at Ole Miss and finished 13-1.

OFFENSE OF THE DECADE: The 2007 Tigers would have gone 14-0 if the defense was as good as the offense. LSU's only two losses in a 12-win season were in overtime, and in each case the offense had put up enough points

See GUILBEAU on Page 4B

Sports in brief

Source tells AP: Redskins will fire Zorn on Monday

The Washington Redskins plan to fire coach **Jim Zorn** on Monday, an official within the NFL told The Associated Press.

The Redskins planned to make the move on the day after the end of a disappointing regular season. Washington struggled early despite a weak schedule and finished 4-12 after losing 23-20 in Sunday's finale against the San Diego Chargers.

Zorn

The official spoke to the AP on Sunday on condition of anonymity because no formal announcement has been made.

"I would not even comment on that," Zorn said after Sunday's game. "There are a lot of things, I'm sure, out there as far as stories. There already has been. So I get that. I'm working on our team meeting, our offseason schedule, and until I'm told that I'm on any other effort, I'm getting ready."

Zorn's dismissal has been expected for months. The front office stripped him of his play-calling duties in late October, and owner **Dan Snyder** has interviewed assistant coach **Jerry Gray** for the job, according to the Fritz Pollard Alliance, which monitors minority hiring in the NFL.

Gray's interview was an effort to comply with the Rooney Rule, which requires that teams consider a minority candidate for the head coaching position. If the NFL deems that the Rooney Rule has been satisfied, the Redskins are free to act quickly to hire a replacement for Zorn. Former Denver Broncos coach **Mike Shanahan** is considered the favorite.

Zorn's replacement will be Washington's seventh coach since Snyder bought the team in 1999. Playing a substantial part in the decision will be **Bruce Allen**, who was hired as the general manager last month.

Only on the Web

UL Blog
Daily Advertiser writer **Joshua Parrott** keeps fans of Ragin' Cajuns athletics up to date with all things UL with his daily blog.

For these features and more, go to theadvertiser.com.

Get breaking sports on your cell phone
Sign up @theadvertiser.com/textme

GetPublished
Share your news, photos and events

E-mail: sports@theadvertiser.com
Call: 289-6303
Fax: 371-3341
Mail: The Daily Advertiser
1100 Bertrand Drive
Lafayette, LA 70506

WEEK 17 SCOREBOARD

Buffalo	**30**	**Chicago**	**37**	**Minnesota**	**44**	**Houston**	**34**	**Kansas City**	**44**	**Green Bay**	**33**	**Tennessee**	**17**
Indianapolis	7	Detroit	23	N.Y. Giants	7	New England	27	Denver	24	Arizona	7	Seattle	13
Cleveland	**23**	**Pittsburgh**	**30**	**Atlanta**	**20**	**Dallas**	**24**	**Baltimore**	**21**	San Diego	23	**N.Y. Jets**	**37**
Jacksonville	17	Miami	24	Tampa Bay	10	Philadelphia	0	Oakland	13	**Washington**	**20**	Cincinnati	0

FOR HOME DELIVERY, CALL 800-259-8852

IT'S ON NOW!

SAINTS MAKE STATEMENT IN LANDSLIDE WIN

By Brady Aymond

NEW ORLEANS — When tailback Reggie Bush emerged from a cloud of smoke in the New Orleans Saints tunnel, brandishing a black baseball bat, it wasn't just a symbolic gesture.

It was a promise.

The message Bush and the Saints were sending was that it's playoff time, and it's time to bring the wood.

And bring it they did.

The Saints brushed off a haymaker from the Arizona

Cardinals on the opening play of the game, then came back with a flurry of punches. And by the end of the third quarter, the Cardinals were waving the white flag.

Just like that, the 13-0 Saints are back and marching into the NFC Championship game with a convincing 45-14 win over the Cardinals before a capacity crowd of 70,149 in the Superdome.

"It's been a season of firsts in a lot of ways," said Saints quarterback Drew Brees, who threw for 247 yards and three touchdowns. "This will be the first NFC Championship game played here and this city deserves it.

"The Who Dat Nation deserves it."

After surprising the team with

the signing of fan-favorite Deuce McAllister to lead the team out and serve as the honorary game captain, Saints coach Sean Payton took it a step further at the team meeting Friday night.

He gave each player a black baseball bat, with the date of Saturday's game and the phrase "Bring the Wood" airbrushed on it.

"Just something we do as a team every once in a while," Payton said. "We've got different themes that we'll use. We thought this was a game we needed to play very physical."

The Saints apparently received the message as they played quite possibly their most physical first half of the season, jumping out to a 35-

14 lead and in the process knocked two starters — safety Antrel Rolle and cornerback Dominique Rodgers-Cromartie — out of the game and sent another — quarterback Kurt Warner — to the locker room prematurely before halftime.

"We wanted to go in and be a lot more physical than them," Saints defensive end Will Smith said. "That was the approach — bring the wood."

It was only appropriate that Bush was the one to carry the bat out onto the field, considering the type of impact he had on the game.

Bush rushed for 84 yards, including a 46-yard touchdown run, caught four passes for 24 yards and added an 83-yard punt return for a

JANUARY 16, 2010

DIVISION PLAYOFF

Saints vs. Cardinals

W 45-14

they gave it right back as Randall Gay stripped the ball from Jerheme Urban after a catch-and-run that covered 28 yards.

The Saints opportunistic defense jumped on the loose ball and the offense turned it into a 14-7 lead as Brees hooked up with Jeremy Shockey for a 17-yard touchdown pass.

"He hit the big sluggo route that took us real close, then he had the touchdown catch," Payton said of Shockey. "He's just another dimension. We used a bunch of different personnel groupings."

The Cardinals' offense sputtered on their next possession, going three-and-out to turn it back over to the Saints.

Bush made sure it hurt as he took the handoff from Brees, broke a tackle at the line of scrimmage, then found a hole in the defense en route to a 46-yard touchdown run and a 21-7 Saints lead.

Arizona finally got its offense going in the second quarter, but not without being aided by a personal foul penalty on the Saints after Warner threw an interception.

Warner's pass intended for Steve Breaston was intercepted by Darren Sharper, but the pick was nullified due to a roughing the passer penalty on Scott Shanle.

Six plays later, Chris "Beanie"

touchdown in leading the Saints to their most complete effort since late November.

"He (Payton) didn't know I

ABOVE: The Saints offense huddles before a play. *Leslie Westbrook/The Daily Advertiser*

OPPOSITE: Saints fans show their spirit as the Saints defeat the Cardinals. *Leslie Westbrook/The Daily Advertiser*

was going to bring it out," Bush said of bringing the bat out during pre-game introductions. "It's not something you do every week. I think coach Payton has some things he likes to do for certain weeks.

"It just symbolizes being the aggressive team all day and giving them hell."

The bat nearly backfired as it was the Cardinals that came out as the

aggressor, scoring on the first play from scrimmage as Tim Hightower found a seam in the defense and raced 70 yards for a 7-0 lead just 19 seconds into the game.

But the Saints remained calm and Brees engineered a 10-play, 72-yard drive to tie the game at 7-7 on Lynell Hamilton's 1-yard run.

The next time Kurt Warner and the Cardinals touched the ball,

Wells capped off a 9-play, 80-yard drive with a 4-yard touchdown run to cut the lead to 21-14.

But as quickly as the Cardinals cut into the lead, the Saints went back up by 14 as Pierre Thomas executed a perfect flea-flicker, tossing the ball back to Brees, who then found a wide-open Devery Henderson for a 44-yard touchdown and a 28-14 lead.

"He just made me look good," Henderson said. "He made a helluva throw away from the defender, and it was just up to me to make the adjustment and make the play."

The Saints then put the game away on the Cards' next possession as Will Smith picked off a Warner pass deep inside Cardinals' territory.

Brees made it a 35-14 lead with a 2-yard touchdown pass to Marques Colston.

"In the playoffs, especially, it's a game of momentum and a game of inches," said Warner, who had a sub-par day with 205 yards on a 17-

RIGHT: Cardinals running back Tim Hightower is tackled by Saints defenders Sedrick Ellis, top to bottom, Roman Harper, Jonathan Vilma and Scott Fujita.
Leslie Westbrook/The Daily Advertiser

OPPOSITE: Saints wide receiver Marques Colston makes a leaping catch in front of Cardinals cornerback Bryant McFadden.
Leslie Westbrook/The Daily Advertiser

of-26 slate before giving way to Matt Leinart in the fourth quarter.

"We knew coming in how good this football team was. And when you play a team in their place, you just can't make mistakes."

Garrett Hartley's 43-yard field goal on the Saints' opening possession of the third quarter made it 38-14. Then Bush put the exclamation point on the victory

....

ABOVE: Saints wide receiver Courtney Roby attempts to outrun Cardinals running back Jason Wright. *Leslie Westbrook/ The Daily Advertiser*

LEFT: Saints running back Pierre Thomas eludes Cardinals linebacker Chike Okeafor to gain a few more yards in the second half. *Denny Culbert/The Daily Advertiser*

OPPOSITE: Saints quarterback Drew Brees looks to pass. *Leslie Westbrook/ The Daily Advertiser*

with an 83-yard punt return for a touchdown to make it 45-14.

Bush continued to shine in the postseason, as he did in 2006 when the Saints last advanced to the NFC Championship game.

"He's as healthy as he's been," Payton said after the win against Arizona. "He was something today. You saw it not only on the punt return, but on the long touchdown run. He played real well today."

So, after answering questions about the team's struggles for the last month, the Saints are now one win away from achieving their goal from the outset — making it to Miami.

"We all see the team that won 13 games in a row, not the team that struggled against the Cowboys, then had one get away from us against Tampa," Brees said. "You can look at the 13-0 Saints or the team that finished losing the last three.

"We know that we are the 13-0 Saints and we played like that today." ⚜

....

RIGHT: Saints wide receiver Devery Henderson makes a touchdown catch in the end zone in front of Cardinals cornerback Bryant McFadden. *Leslie Westbrook/The Daily Advertiser*

OPPOSITE: Saints wide receiver Devery Henderson hands his touchdown ball to a fan. *Leslie Westbrook/The Daily Advertiser*

WARNER MAY HAVE PLAYED FINAL GAME

By Bob Tompkins

NEW ORLEANS — Kurt Warner may have played the final game of his splendid NFL career January 16, 2010 in the Louisiana Superdome, but he wasn't ready to announce anything.

His defending NFC champions lost to the New Orleans Saints, 45-14, in the Superdome, and Warner, at age 38, absorbed a brutal blindside block from defensive end Bobby McCray

after he had a pass intercepted by Will Smith, the other Saints defensive end, in the second quarter.

That sent him to the sidelines for the remainder of the first half, including the Cardinals' last possession of the second quarter. Although he returned to play in the third quarter, he sat out the fourth quarter while Matt Leinart did mop-up duty with his team down, 38-14, after three periods.

"You know, a big hit like that makes you think twice about playing this game," Warner said with a laugh. "I have a lot of ideas in my head (about retiring), but what

I need to do now is just get away. And by that I mean get away from the season and talk it over with my wife and kids — especially my wife.

"As I've told you guys a million times before," he went on, "that's something I will think about and answer later. I don't think it will be a long, drawn-out process. I think it's something I will discuss with my family and inform the organization about what I plan to do as soon as I have time to think about it."

We've all been through this kind of talk before from Brett Favre, again and again and again, but I have a feeling if Warner decides

to retire, he will do so for good. I wouldn't be surprised if Warner's wife, who was in attendance Saturday, encourages him to walk away while he still can walk.

Early Doucet, the LSU product from St. Martinville, said he didn't like it when Warner was being attended to as he lay on the Superdome turf.

"He's our leader, but we don't like it when he or any of our guys are injured," said Doucet, who led the Cardinals in receiving Saturday with eight catches for 68 yards. "Matt stepped in and, even though we didn't score, showed he could lead our offense down the field."

Doucet said the Saints defense, which ranked near the bottom of the NFL after some poor late-season games, did a good job shutting down the Cardinals' offense with the help of some returning healthy players.

"They've got some veteran guys

....

LEFT: Saints linebacker Jonathan Vilma (51) gets a hand on Cardinals quarterback Kurt Warner. *Leslie Westbrook/The Daily Advertiser*

OPPOSITE LEFT: Saints wide receiver Marques Colston runs with the ball. *Leslie Westbrook/The Daily Advertiser*

OPPOSITE RIGHT: Saints defensive tackle Sedrick Ellis puts pressure on Cardinals quarterback Kurt Warner in the second half. *Denny Culbert/The Daily Advertiser*

and they know about these types of games," said Doucet, who played in front of 25 to 30 relatives after enjoying a dinner at Brennan's with family members Friday.

....

ABOVE LEFT: Saints defensive end Will Smith runs with the ball after making an interception. *Leslie Westbrook/The Daily Advertiser*

ABOVE RIGHT: Saints defenders Jonathan Vilma (51) and Randall Gay chase Cardinals running back Tim Hightower out of bounds in the second half. Hightower gained no yards on the play which brought up a fourth down which the Cardinals failed to covert into a first down. *Denny Culbert/The Daily Advertiser*

LEFT: Saints running back Reggie Bush points back at Cardinals defenders as he returns a punt for a touchdown in the second half. *Denny Culbert/The Daily Advertiser*

OPPOSITE: Saints running back Reggie Bush returns a punt for a touchdown. *Denny Culbert/The Daily Advertiser*

Arizona's defense, which allowed Green Bay to score on its last five possessions of the second half (including overtime) last week, allowed the Saints to score on five of their six possessions in the first half Saturday.

At 6-feet, cornerback Bryant McFadden, a five-year veteran from Florida State, was beat twice on scoring plays in the second period — once on a 44-yard flea flicker by Devery Henderson, who turned around on the run a step ahead of McFadden to catch the touchdown pass from Saints quarterback Drew Brees.

Later in the first half, he was beat twice on the final two plays of another Saints scoring drive by 6-foot-4 Marques Colston — a 15-yard pass to the 2 and a 2-yard pass

for the score.

"They played at a very high level," McFadden said of the Saints. "They were in good rhythm. "(Colston) is a good receiver. He knows how to use his body and his big frame and outstanding hands."

The guys in red who almost won last year's Super Bowl gave due praise to their conquering foes.

Was this a passing of the torch, from Warner to Brees, from last year's NFC champion to a team that will try to become this year's NFC champ?

We'll see soon enough. ✠

RIGHT: Saints quarterback Drew Brees watches his pass float to running back Pierre Thomas in the second half. *Denny Culbert/ The Daily Advertiser*

OPPOSITE: Saints running back Pierre Thomas slips by Cardinals linebacker Monty Biesel. *Denny Culbert/The Daily Advertiser*

ABOVE: Saints tight end Jeremy Shockey celebrates a touchdown.
Leslie Westbrook/The Daily Advertiser

TOP LEFT: A fan holds up a sign. *Leslie Westbrook/The Daily Advertiser*

LEFT: Cardinals wide receiver Early Doucet is run down by Saints linebacker Scott Shanle.
Leslie Westbrook/The Daily Advertiser

OPPOSITE: Saints free safety Darren Sharper grabs an interception intended for Cardinals wide receiver Steve Breaston. *Leslie Westbrook/The Daily Advertiser*

ABOVE: Saints middle linebacker Jonathan Vilma celebrates after the game.
Leslie Westbrook/The Daily Advertiser

TOP: Saints free safety Darren Sharper cheers to the crowd. *Leslie Westbrook/ The Daily Advertiser*

RIGHT: Saints owner Tom Benson and his wife Gayle congratulate tight end Jeremy Shockey after the game. *Leslie Westbrook/ The Daily Advertiser*

OPPOSITE: Saints nose tackle Remi Ayo-dele (92) celebrates with DeMario Pressley after winning the game. *Leslie Westbrook/ The Daily Advertiser*

HOW 'BOUT DAT?

SAINTS ARE SUPER BOWL BOUND!

By Brady Aymond

NEW ORLEANS — Sometimes, even Saints need a little divine intervention.

On January 24, 2010 in the Louisiana Superdome, the New Orleans Saints needed more than just a little.

With the score tied 28-all and the seconds ticking down in the NFC Championship game, the Minnesota Vikings marched into Saints territory and appeared poised to let Ryan Longwell attempt a game-winning field goal.

....

OPPOSITE: Saints quarterback Drew Brees smiles as confetti falls after the NFC Championship game. *Leslie Westbrook/ The Daily Advertiser*

Then, fate intervened.

First, the Vikings were called for an illegal participation penalty to turn a 50-yard attempt into a 55-yard attempt.

Then, as Minnesota quarterback Brett Favre attempted to get those yards back, Saints cornerback Tracy Porter stepped in front of his pass to intercept it and send the game into overtime.

The Saints won the coin toss in overtime and marched into Vikings territory and into Super Bowl XLIV as kicker Garrett Hartley nailed a 40-yard field goal to set off a Mardi Gras-like celebration as the Saints beat the Vikings, 31-28, to win the NFC Championship before a franchise-record crowd of 71,276 at the Superdome.

"It's hard to come up here and really talk about the significance of this group of guys in that locker room and the significance of this win," Saints coach Sean Payton said after the game. "I'm proud of them, proud of our fans and it's a pretty special feeling."

Pierre Thomas came up big in the overtime period, first returning the kickoff 40 yards to give the Saints good field position to start. Then he went over the top on a fourth-and-one at the Minnesota 43-yard line to continue the drive.

The Saints got down to the Minnesota 34 on a pass from Drew Brees to Robert Meachem, then got a big pass interference call to put them down to the 22-yard line to bring out

Hartley for the game-winner.

"I have to say absolutely this is the best game I've ever been in," Thomas said. "It was an exciting game. In the beginning it went back and forth. They'd make plays and we'd make plays."

The game was dominated throughout by the Minnesota offense, which churned out 475 yards and held the ball for nearly 37 minutes.

On the flip side, the Saints could muster only 235 yards through regulation, but their defense came up big when it needed to, forcing six fumbles by the Vikings and picking off Favre twice. Four of the Vikings' five turnovers came in the second half, and most came when Minnesota was threatening to score.

Miami native Jonathan Vilma had one of the interceptions, and recovered another fumble, as the Saints advanced to the franchise's first-ever Super Bowl appearance.

"It's great to go home the right way," from Super Bowl XLIV Vilma said of making a trip to Miami. "I've been saying that ever since I got selected to the Pro Bowl that I wanted to go home the right way. This is the only way to go."

The game was about as strange a back-and-forth shootout as you could imagine as the teams took turns matching each other on the scoreboard, but did so in different methods.

The Vikings' four scoring drives covered an average of 72.5 yards while the Saints five scoring drives averaged 44.6 yards.

"This was such an up-and-down game, it seemed like no call was going our way," Saints tailback Reggie Bush said. "In the end we finally got a few calls going our way."

The first quarter set the tone for things to come as the Vikings (13-5) and Saints combined for 21 points, with the Vikings taking a quick 14-7 lead at the end of one quarter of play.

Favre, who threw for 310 yards on a 28-of-46 slate, engineered drives of 80 and 73 yards, while Drew Brees was able to put together a 76-yard drive of his own as the first quarter resembled

the shootout that many anticipated.

The two offenses started firing blanks after that, exchanging punts before Bush re-ignited the Saints. Bush hauled in a pass over the middle from Brees and raced 28 yards into Minnesota territory.

A few plays later, Brees had all day to find Devery Henderson in the back corner of the end zone from nine yards out to tie the game at 14-14 after Hartley's extra point.

From that point, the defenses took over and the game remained tied until late in the second quarter. The Saints appeared poised to get the ball to end the half, but those plans blew up when Bush muffed a punt at his own 10-yard line.

Minnesota's Eric Frampton was there to force the fumble and teammate Kenny Onatolu fell on the loose ball to put the Vikings in position for a go-ahead score with 1:13 left in the half.

Fortune smiled on the Saints two plays later, though, as a handoff from Favre to Peterson never got to its intended target and fell to the Superdome turf. Scott Fujita was there

to pounce on the loose ball to thwart that drive and allow the Saints to run out the remaining time on the clock.

"It's kind of a blur right now," Payton said. "I know we came up with a turnover margin that was pretty significant, 5-1, and we win by a field goal, you have to credit Minnesota. That's unusual.

"There's time when we've given up some yardage this year, but when you look at the takeaways now and the ones we got, I thought the one we got at the end of the half was significant."

The Saints came out in the second half with guns blazing as Courtney Roby returned the opening kickoff 61 yards into Minnesota territory.

Brees and the Saints offense covered the remaining 37 yards in four

plays to take a 21-14 lead on Thomas' 9-yard touchdown run.

But the Saints offense stalled and the Vikings' offense spent the entire second half playing in New Orleans territory, only to come away with just enough points to force overtime.

The Vikings answered the Saints touchdown with another 80-yard drive in 10 plays. The Saints blew a big opportunity in the drive, however, as Peterson had fumbled the football and two Saints players converged on the loose ball.

But Scott Shanle couldn't get a handle on it, and the Vikings Naufahu Tahi won the scramble to maintain possession.

Favre then hit tight end Visanthe Shiancoe with a pair of 20-yard strikes

THE DAILY ADVERTISER

Monday, January 25, 2010 · theadvertiser.com · 75 cents ★

INSIDETODAY

Haiti death toll tops 150,000

The Haitian government
says 150,000 bodies have
been recovered, not counting
untold other thousands still
under the quake debris or car-
ried off by relatives. **Page 9A**

State cuts affect recreation areas

The head of the state
Department of Culture,
Recreation and Tourism says
the public shouldn't feel the
impact of budget cuts, but
some services will be limited.
Page 7A

To our readers

Because of production
issues, delivery of some cop-
ies of The Daily Advertiser
may have been delayed today.
This is not the fault of your
carrier.

**Your best bets right
to your cell phone**

Sign up
**the
advertiser**
.com/textme

ROOFING
LOUISIANA

INSIDETODAY

Accent	**10A**	Lottery	**2A**
Celebrity		Movies	**3A**
Cipher	**11A**	Nation &	
Comics	**8B**	World	**9A**
Crossword	**8B**	Obituaries	**6A**
Dear Abby	**9B**	On TV	**9B**
		Opinions	**4A**
Growth &		Religion	
Business	**8A**	Sudoku	**11A**
Horoscope	**11A**	Sports	**1B**

GetPublished

Share your news,
photos and events

E-mail: news@theadvertiser.com
Call: 289NEWS
Fax: 289-6443
Mail: 1100 Bertrand Drive
Lafayette, LA 70506

A Gannett Newspaper
Lafayette, Louisiana
Copyright 2010

Full coverage of the Superdome victory in Sports, Page 1B

NEW ORLEANS 31 ● MINNESOTA 28

BELIEVE IT!

Saints quarterback Drew Brees holds the trophy after defeating the Vikings 31-28 in overtime in the NFC Championship football game Sunday at the Superdome in New Orleans. The Saints will take on the Indianapolis Colts in the Super Bowl on Feb. 7 in Miami.

Leslie Westbrook/lwestbrook@theadvertiser.com

■ Acadiana fans rejoice in
victory, join rush to buy Saints
championship T-shirts.
Page 3A

■ For Brees and the boys, it all
came down to this. Get full
coverage and analysis of the
game. **Page 1B**

■ Continue the celebration. See
photo galleries from the Dome,
talk to other local fans, watch
videos at **theadvertiser.com**.

theadvertiser.com: Weather . Jobs . Cars . Homes . Shopping . Classifieds

---

to set up a 1-yard TD run by Peterson to tie the score. Peterson ran for 122 yards and three touchdowns in the contest.

On the Vikings' opening possession of the fourth quarter, Percy Harvin fumbled the football and a scramble ensued. Eventually, New Orleans defensive tackle Remi Ayodele came up with the football and returned it down to the 7-yard line.

Three plays later, the Saints went up 28-21 on Bush's 5-yard touchdown reception from Brees. Initially, the play was ruled down at the 1-yard line, but Payton threw the challenge flag after replay showed Bush got the ball across the goalline.

Minnesota tied the game two possessions later, aided by a pass interference call on Porter in the end zone to set up another 1-yard touchdown run by Peterson.

The Saints got the ball back on the ensuing kickoff, but again failed to do anything with it and had to punt it back to Minnesota with 2:37 left in the game.

After a big third-down conversion on a 10-yard pass to Berrian, Favre got the Vikings into Saints territory with a 20-yard pass to Sidney Rice. The Vikings got down to the 33-yard

....

ABOVE: Fans dressed as popes cheer on the Saints. *Leslie Westbrook/The Daily Advertiser*

RIGHT: Saints fans cheer before the start of the game. *Denny Culbert/The Daily Advertiser*

line with a little more than a minute to play in the game, and appeared ready to settle for a Ryan Longwell field goal attempt to win the game.

The Vikings broke the huddle with 12 players, though, on a third-and-10 play, which resulted in a 5-yard penalty to back it up to the 38-yard line. On the next play, Favre attempted to throw the ball across his body to Rice, but Porter stepped in front of the pass for the interception and to send the game into OT.

Once in overtime, the Saints won the toss and took the ball. Thomas provided the big boost as he took the kickoff one yard deep and returned it 40 yards to the 39-yard line. The Saints methodically drove into Vikings territory, aided by a defensive holding penalty on a third-and-six incomplete pass to Marques Colston.

Later in the drive, Brees hit Henderson for a 9-yard gain down to the Vikings' 43-yard line. But the play came up one yard short and the Saints

RIGHT: Saints tight end David Thomas celebrates. *Denny Culbert/The Daily Advertiser*

OPPOSITE LEFT: Saints running back Reggie Bush falls forward for extra yardage as he is tackled by Vikings Madieu Williams. *Leslie Westbrook/The Daily Advertiser*

OPPOSITE RIGHT: Saints running back Pierre Thomas runs the ball. *Leslie Westbrook/ The Daily Advertiser*

had to go for it on fourth-and-one.

The call went to Thomas, who went over the top to get the first down with a 1-yard gain. On the next play, the Saints were fortunate again, as Minnesota's Ben Leber was flagged for pass interference to put the Saints in field goal range at the 29-yard line.

A 12-yard pass from Brees to Meachem got them a little closer and set the stage for Hartley's game-winner.

"I just knew when it came off my foot that it was going to split the pipes," Hartley said. "It was fate for this team to head to Miami to head to the Super Bowl this year. I'm just honored to be a part of it." ✣

....

RIGHT: Vikings running back Adrian Peterson drags Saints cornerback Tracy Porter behind him. *Denny Culbert/The Daily Advertiser*

OPPOSITE LEFT: Saints linebacker Scott Fujita bows to the crowd after making a play. *Denny Culbert/The Daily Advertiser*

OPPOSITE TOP RIGHT: Saints running back Reggie Bush celebrates with Devery Henderson after scoring a touchdown. *Denny Culbert/The Daily Advertiser*

OPPOSITE BOTTOM RIGHT: Saints quarterback Drew Brees throws a pass. *Denny Culbert/The Daily Advertiser*

IT'S OFFICIAL AFTER DRAMATIC WIN: THESE SAINTS ARE S-U-P-E-R

By Glenn Guilbeau

NEW ORLEANS — It is a good thing Dave Dixon — the father of the Superdome — did not come to this one.

Dixon, the 86-year-old mastermind who convinced state officials to build the dome four decades ago, said Saturday that he had attended his final Saints game last week when his beloved team advanced to Sunday night's NFC Championship Game with a win over Arizona in the dome.

"I have a mild heart condition and I tire very easily," Dixon said. "I had a mild setback at that game and will not be going to the game Sunday night. I get too excited. I've seen my last game in the dome."

Good call, Dave, but you missed the greatest one ever in your building.

"Oh, how sweet it is," the forever voice of the dome Jerry Romig said seconds after Garrett Hartley kicked a 40-year-old field goal in overtime to give the Saints a 31-28 victory over Minnesota and send the 43-year-old franchise to its first Super Bowl.

And right then, they cued up, "Oh When The Saints Go Marching In."

Romig just kept repeating, "SUPER BOWL ... SUPER BOWL ... SUPER BOWL."

The Saints will play Indianapolis and New Orleans native quarterback Peyton Manning in Miami on Sunday, Feb. 7.

"Congratulations, Saints," Romig

....

OPPOSITE: Courtney Roby runs the ball. *Leslie Westbrook/The Daily Advertiser*

BELOW: Fans cheer during the game. *Denny Culbert/The Daily Advertiser*

roared. "You finished strong!" That's what the T-Shirts say that Saints and Saints fans alike have been wearing for weeks.

Dixon and his condition would not have been alone had he made the game. There were likely thousands whose heart skipped a beat at least once a quarter or lodged in their throats every few minutes in the Dramadome's first-ever NFC Championship Game.

Minnesota took a 7-0 lead behind 40-year-old legend Brett Favre, who admitted he was a closet Saints fan early this week. Then it was quarterback Drew Brees' turn, and he led the Saints to a 7-7 tie. Minnesota went back up 14-7. Then it was 14-14 at the half before New Orleans went up 21-14 in the third quarter, and it got tied again at 21 in the third and then at 28 in the fourth and through regulation.

In the end, the Saints got the breaks in a break with tradition. You can spell Karma with an S-A-I-N-T now, or, if you prefer, S-U-P-E-R.

Either way, it's not a four-letter word any more because the C-U-R-S-E has been virtually completely lifted.

Just when they needed it most, the New Orleans Saints — hexed for most of their 43-year history — got the breaks and the bounces and the rolls, and THEY are going to the Super Bowl. Check out hell before

you get to heaven in two weeks in Miami, Saints fans, because I hear it's below freezing.

This time — at last — the other team screwed the pooch.

Favre had the ball last in regulation with enough time to score, and frighteningly the stage appeared set for one more comeback by the ancient gladiator from nearby Kiln, Miss. He and the Vikings took over at their 21 with two minutes to play. Gradually he matriculated Minnesota to the New Orleans 33-yard line with 19 seconds to play for a 50-yard field goal. Saint fans saw it all disintegrating.

But Minnesota inexplicably broke the huddle with 12 men, and suddenly its purple and gold trim was reminiscent of a team an hour from here. That meant a five-yard penalty, and Favre would have to pass. He did, and Saints cornerback Tracy Porter intercepted and returned it 26 yards to midfield. That was Minnesota's fourth turnover of the second half. Thank you, and bless YOU boys.

The Saints tried two passes, but on came overtime.

After New Orleans won the toss, they played "The Saints Are Coming," and they did, but it was not easy.

After a 40-yard kickoff return by Pierre Thomas set the Saints up at

its 39, the movement was slow. On third and 10, Brees was rushed and threw desperately for wide receiver Devery Henderson. He caught it, but he only got nine yards. On fourth and one, Thomas leaped for the first down. A critical pass interference call against Minnesota linebacker Ben Leber pushed the drive to the Minnesota 29 and into field goal range.

But tailback Reggie Bush lost five yards on the next play to the 34. That would be a 51-yard kick. So on second down, Brees found Robert Meachem for 12 yards to the 22.

On fourth and three, Hartley came out for the 40-yard field goal. Minnesota called a timeout to make him think about the 37-yard try he missed to lose to Tampa Bay last month. During the timeout, he spoke to coach Sean Payton.

Then he drilled it. And it was over.

A decade ago when the Saints won their first playoff game thanks to a fumbled punt return by St. Louis, voice of the Saints Jim Henderson proclaimed, "There is a God."

On this night, New Orleans found out there is a heaven.

RIGHT: Saints wide receiver Marques Colston makes a catch. *Denny Culbert/ The Daily Advertiser*

"See you in Miami everybody," Romig said.

And they cued up Kool and the Gang's "Celebration," which came out in 1980 when the Saints went 1-15. They are 15-3 now.

"We're gonna have a good time tonight," Kool and the Gang sang.

"Let's celebrate. It's alright." ✦

....

RIGHT: Vikings wide receiver Darius Reynaud faces a group of Saints defenders on a kickoff return. *Denny Culbert/The Daily Advertiser*

OPPOSITE LEFT: Vikings running back Adrian Peterson is brought down by a group of Saints defenders. *Denny Culbert/ The Daily Advertiser*

OPPOSITE TOP: Saints defensive coordinator Gregg Williams watches from the sideline. *Denny Culbert/The Daily Advertiser*

OPPOSITE BOTTOM: Saints fans show their emotions during the game. *Denny Culbert/The Daily Advertiser*

ABOVE: Vikings quarterback Brett Favre fumbles the ball after a hit from Saints cornerback Jabari Greer, left. *Leslie Westbrook/ The Daily Advertiser*

RIGHT: Saints defensive tackle Remi Ayodele picks up a ball fumbled by Vikings quarterback Brett Favre. *Leslie Westbrook/ The Daily Advertiser*

FAR RIGHT: New Orleans Saints running back Pierre Thomas dives over the Minnesota defense for a first down in the fourth quarter that helped the Saints defeat the Vikings. *Denny Culbert/The Daily Advertiser*

OPPOSITE TOP: Saints backup quarterback and field goal holder Mark Brunell, left, and David Thomas hug kicker Garrett Hartley after he kicked the game-winning field goal. *Leslie Westbrook/The Daily Advertiser*

OPPOSITE BOTTOM: Saints running back Reggie Bush, left, celebrates with Sedrick Ellis after the game. *Denny Culbert/ The Daily Advertiser*

LEFT: Saints head coach Sean Payton holds up the NFC Championship trophy. *Leslie Westbrook/The Daily Advertiser*

OPPOSITE: Saints quarterback Drew Brees celebrates with fans. *Leslie Westbrook/ The Daily Advertiser*

ABOVE: Saints owner Tom Benson, center, holds up the NFC Championship trophy with players and staff. *Leslie Westbrook/ The Daily Advertiser*

TOP: Vikings quarterback Brett Favre congratulates Saints quarterback Drew Brees. *Denny Culbert/The Daily Advertiser*

SIMPLY SUPER

DESTINY'S TEAM RIDES ARM OF BREES TO HISTORIC WIN

By Brady Aymond

MIAMI — Four and a half years ago, the fight shown by the city of New Orleans was an inspiration to Drew Brees and his teammates.

Here Sunday night, Brees and the New Orleans Saints gave that inspiration back many times over.

Brees, who came to New Orleans as a reject in a time when the city was at a low point after Hurricane Katrina, completed 32-of-39 passes for 288 yards and two touchdowns, including the game-winner to

....

OPPOSITE: The Saints celebrate in the end zone after Jeremy Shockey, holding the ball, scored in the fourth quarter to give the Saints the lead in the game.
Brad Kemp/The Daily Advertiser

Jeremy Shockey with 5:42 left to lift the Saints to a 31-17 win over the Indianapolis Colts to be crowned Super Bowl XLIV champions.

Brees was named the game's MVP after completing 82.1 percent of his passes, which is second-highest in Super Bowl history behind Phil Simms' record of 88 percent in Super Bowl XXI.

With tears welling up in his eyes, Brees held his 1-year old son Baylen and whispered in his ear while pointing to the crowd.

Chances are his son will not remember anything from this magical night in Miami. But he'll have people reminding him every day for the rest of his life.

"We love you, we love you, baby,"

Brees said. "The Who Dat nation allowed us to be here. What you did is you gave us the strength and the courage to know that we could do it. This championship is for you, New Orleans."

The Saints (16-3) adopted the grit displayed by their city and regions' residents following one of the worst natural disasters to hit an American city.

And that never-quit attitude was on display again Sunday night, as the Saints twice rallied from deficits in the contest.

"Not only did the organization come back and city come back, we had a core group of players that came in that year as free agents and we all looked at each other and said 'We're

going to rebuild together,'" Brees said. "And that's what we've done the last four years. And this is a culmination of all that belief and that faith."

The Saints were still in tourist mode in the first quarter, doing a lot of watching as the Colts took their first two possessions down the field for a 10-0 lead.

After the Saints went three-and-out on their opening possession, Peyton Manning and the Colts drove 53 yards in 11 plays to take a 3-0 lead on Matt Stover's 38-yard field goal.

The Saints had to punt again on their next possession and pinned the Colts at their own 4-yard line. But Indy went on a Super Bowl-record tying 96-yard scoring drive to take a 10-0 lead on Manning's 19-yard TD pass to Pierre Garcon.

As soon as the second quarter started, the game swung in the Saints' favor.

After gaining only 36 yards in the first quarter, the Saints rolled up 143 in the second quarter and held the ball for nearly 13 minutes.

But the Saints could only get two Garrett Hartley field goals — one from 46 and another from 44 as time expired.

The Saints had gotten down to the Colts' 1-yard line, but Mike Bell slipped for no gain on third down and Pierre Thomas was stuffed by Gary Brackett for no gain on a fourth-down attempt.

Saints coach Sean Payton wanted to capitalize on the momentum of Hartley's 44-yard field goal to end the half as he went for an onside kick to start the third quarter.

It worked as the Colts weren't expecting it and it bounced off a Colts defender right into Chris Reis' hands. The Saints took advantage, driving down in six plays to take a 13-10 lead on Brees' 16-yard TD pass to Thomas.

"Well, we were going to be aggressive," Payton said. "When you do something like that, you just put it on the players and they were able to execute. It turned out to be a big change of possession and ended with a score."

The unflappable Manning — who threw for 333 yards and a touchdown in the loss — came right back, though, to engineer a 10-play, 76-yard touchdown drive to give the Colts a 17-13 lead on a 4-yard run by Joseph Addai.

But Hartley nailed a 47-yard field goal, then the Saints took advantage of a Stover missed 51-yard field goal

....

ABOVE: Saints fans Richard Romero, left, and Rebecca Holleman of New Orleans enjoy themselves before entering the stadium for Super Bowl XLIV. For years Saints fans covered their heads with paper bags and called themselves the 'Aints. Fans are now celebrating that those years are gone.
Brad Kemp/The Daily Advertiser

RIGHT: The Saints' Roman Harper sizes up the crowd before playing the Colts.
Brad Kemp/The Daily Advertiser

OPPOSITE: Saints fans cheer on their team. For many fans, this season, and the first Super Bowl win, was the Saints' destiny.
Brad Kemp/The Daily Advertiser

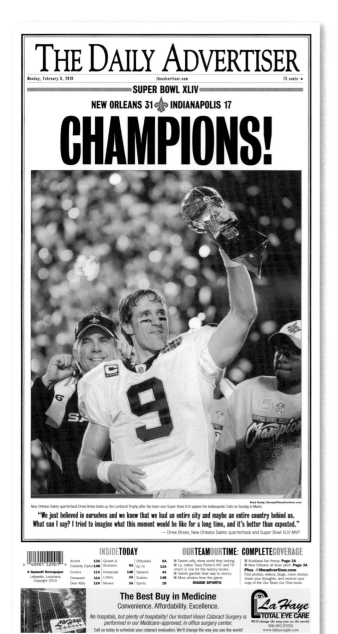

THE DAILY ADVERTISER

Monday, February 8, 2010 · theadvertiser.com · 75 cents ★

SUPER BOWL XLIV

NEW ORLEANS 31 ✦ INDIANAPOLIS 17

CHAMPIONS!

New Orleans Saints quarterback Drew Brees holds up the Lombardi Trophy after the team won Super Bowl XLIV against the Indianapolis Colts on Sunday in Miami.
Brad Kemp/bkemp@theadvertiser.com

"We just believed in ourselves and we knew that we had an entire city and maybe an entire country behind us. What can I say? I tried to imagine what this moment would be like for a long time, and it's better than expected."
— Drew Brees, New Orleans Saints quarterback and Super Bowl XLIV MVP

A Gannett Newspaper
Lafayette, Louisiana
Copyright 2010

INSIDE TODAY

Accent	13A	Growth &		Obituaries	6A
Celebrity Cipher	14B	Business	9A	On TV	12A
Comics	11A	Horoscope	14B	Opinions	4A
Crossword	11A	Lottery	2A	Sudoku	14B
Dear Abby	12A	Movies	3A	Sports	1B

OUR TEAM OUR TIME: COMPLETE COVERAGE

■ Saints rally, show world they belong.
■ La. native Tracy Porter's INT and TD return is one for the history books.
■ Saints gamble their way to victory.
■ More photos from the game.
INSIDE SPORTS

■ Acadiana fan frenzy. **Page 2A**
■ New Orleans at fever pitch. **Page 3A**
Plus, @theadvertiser.com
Find photos, videos, blogs, more stories, share your thoughts, and reserve your copy of the Our Team Our Time book.

The Best Buy in Medicine
Convenience. Affordability. Excellence.

No hospitals, but plenty of hospitality! Our Instant Vision Cataract Surgery is performed in our Medicare-approved, in office surgery center.
Call us today to schedule your cataract evaluation. We'll change the way you see the world!

La Haye
TOTAL EYE CARE
We'll change the way you see the world.
800-892-EYES
www.lahayesight.com

theadvertiser.com : Weather . Jobs . Cars . Homes . Shopping . Classifieds

FEBRUARY 7, 2010

SUPER BOWL

Saints vs. Colts

W 31-17

to drive down for the game-winning touchdown.

The drive covered 59 yards in nine plays and culminated with a 2-yard pass from Brees to Shockey in the endzone.

"It's a great feeling right now," Shockey said. "I don't care about the catch, I just care about the team. Ever since you start playing football, you're dreaming about playing in this game.

"I dreamed and prayed all day and night about being in the situation I'm in right now and that's what happened."

The Saints went for two and got it when Brees' pass to Lance Moore was ruled a catch after instant replay confirmed he had possession of the ball as it crossed the goal line to make it 24-17.

Manning still had time to bring the

Colts back, but Tracy Porter ended that abruptly as he picked off a Manning pass intended for Reggie Wayne and returned it 74 yards for the game-clinching touchdown — the defense's ninth touchdown of the season.

"The coaching staff did a great

....

ABOVE: Saints head coach Sean Payton talks to his team as they warm up. *Brad Kemp/The Daily Advertiser*

TOP RIGHT: Courtney Roby had four kickoff returns for 102 yards in the game. *Brad Kemp/The Daily Advertiser*

BOTTOM RIGHT: Courtney Roby celebrates after making a special teams play during the game. *Brad Kemp/The Daily Advertiser*

OPPOSITE: Saints offensive guard Carl Nicks, right, was part of a New Orleans offensive line that allowed just one sack while collecting 20 first downs and 281 total yards. *Brad Kemp/The Daily Advertiser*

job of preparing us for that route," Porter said. "We knew that (Colts WR Austin) Collie was a guy they usually don't put at number one. We knew he was going to motion down with the inverted split.

"Once he motioned down, we knew number one was going to wide-depart and run to the sticks. I saw him do that, he wide-departed and I jumped the route and the ball came right into my hands."

Manning and the Colts had one last gasp, and Manning tried to make the most of it. He drove the Colts down to the Saints goal line before a fourth-down pass attempt to Wayne went through his hands.

Brees and the Saints offense came back out one last time to run out the remaining seconds and set off a Mardi Gras celebration all along the Gulf Coast and up and down the South Florida Coast.

"Tonight the Super Bowl belongs to the city of New Orleans and their great fans," NFL commissioner Roger Goodell said as he handed the Lombardi Trophy to owner Tom Benson.

Four years, four months and 40

....

RIGHT: Saints linebacker Jonathan Vilma dives for Colts running back Joseph Addai. *Brad Kemp/The Daily Advertiser*

OPPOSITE: The Saints defense goes after Colts wide receiver Pierre Garcon. *Brad Kemp/ The Daily Advertiser*

days after Hurricane Katrina left nothing but hopelessness and despair in her wake, the Saints gave its fans a reason to smile.

"Never give up," Saints safety Darren Sharper said. "That's why we were able to keep fighting this year, because we were always able to look back at our community and see the things that they went through and how they kept fighting, even though, some would say, the world was against them.

"Everyone overlooked them. It's the same with us as a team. Everyone overlooked us in this game, and we used that as motivation." ⚜

LEFT: Malcolm Jenkins celebrates after a huge hit on kickoff coverage. The Saints never allowed the Colts' special teams to be a factor. *Brad Kemp/The Daily Advertiser*

OPPOSITE: Saints receiver Lance Moore avoids defender Melvin Bullitt. *Brad Kemp/ The Daily Advertiser*

FOLLOWING LEFT: Saints linebacker Scott Shanle tackles Colts wide receiver Austin Collie. *Brad Kemp/The Daily Advertiser*

FOLLOWING MIDDLE: The Saints defense brings down Colts running back Chad Simpson. *Brad Kemp/The Daily Advertiser*

FOLLOWING TOP RIGHT: Reggie Bush escapes Colts defender Kelvin Hayden. *Brad Kemp/The Daily Advertiser*

FOLLOWING BOTTOM RIGHT: Running back Reggie Bush escapes a Colts defender. *Brad Kemp/The Daily Advertiser*

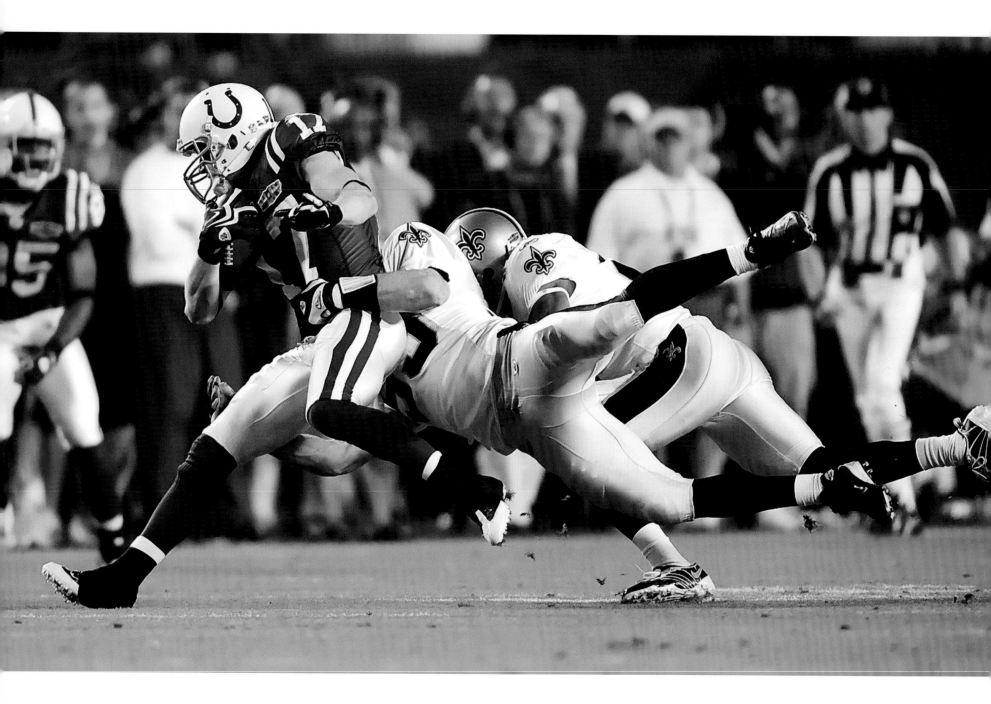

RIGHT: The Saints' Lance Moore moves past defensive back Kelvin Hayden during the game. Moore caught a two-point conversion pass that gave the Saints a 24-17 lead in the fourth quarter. *Brad Kemp/The Daily Advertiser*

OPPOSITE TOP: Saints defenders Jonathan Vilma, from left, Jabari Greer and Randall Gay go after Colts wide receiver Austin Collie. *Brad Kemp/The Daily Advertiser*

OPPOSITE BOTTOM LEFT: The Saints' Randall Gay dives for Colts receiver Austin Collie during Super Bowl XLIV. Gay previously won a Super Bowl ring with the Patriots. *Brad Kemp/The Daily Advertiser*

OPPOSITE BOTTOM RIGHT: Saints quarterback Drew Brees is sacked by Colts defender Dwight Freeney. Freeney whipped Brees to the ground with one hand. *Brad Kemp/The Daily Advertiser*

FOLLOWING LEFT: Saints running back Pierre Thomas is tackled by the Colts defense. Thomas scored on a pass from Drew Brees that gave the Saints their first lead of the game in the third quarter. *Brad Kemp/The Daily Advertiser*

FOLLOWING RIGHT: Saints wide receiver and Opelousas, La., native Devery Henderson avoids Colts defender Antoine Bethea. Henderson had seven receptions for 63 yards. *Brad Kemp/The Daily Advertiser*

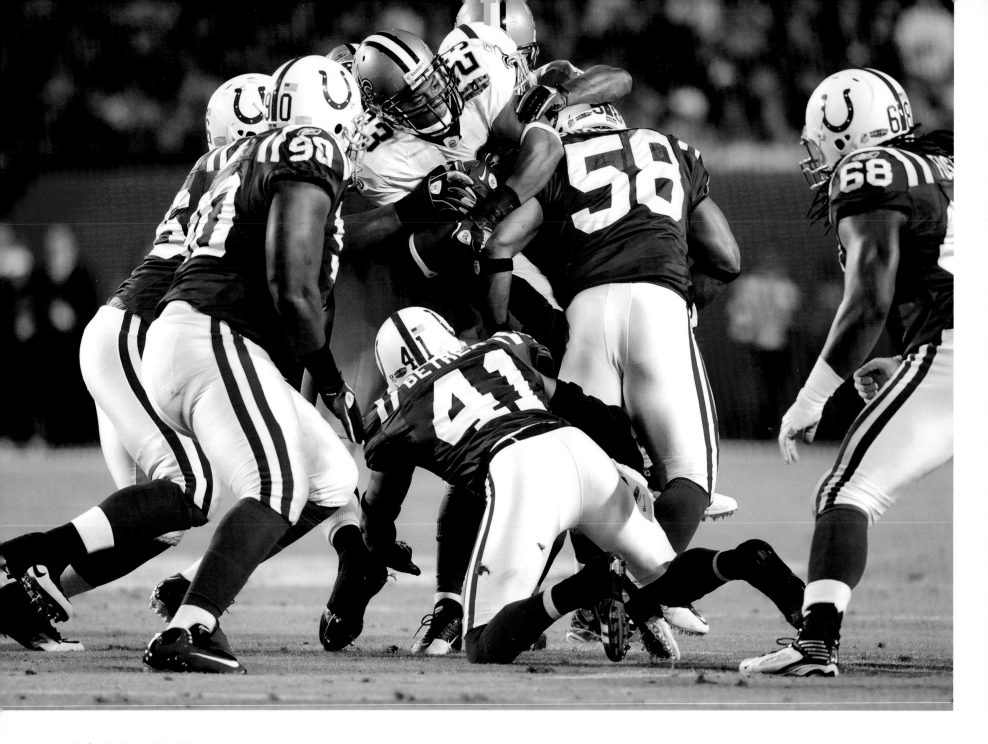

ABOVE: Saints kicker Garrett Hartley makes a kick during Super Bowl XLIV. Hartley set a Super Bowl record by making three field goals of over 40 yards. *Brad Kemp/ The Daily Advertiser*

LEFT: Saints wide receiver Marques Colston avoids the Colts defense as he gains yardage for New Orleans. *Brad Kemp/The Daily Advertiser*

OPPOSITE: Saints wide receiver Robert Meachem shrugs off Colts defender Antoine Bethea. *Brad Kemp/The Daily Advertiser*

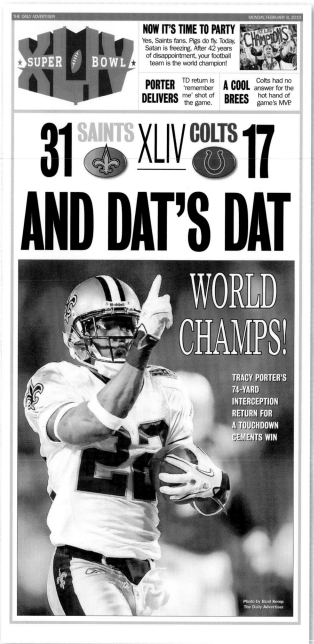

PORTER INTERCEPTION WAS ONE TO REMEMBER

By Glenn Guilbeau

MIAMI — A Hoosier from Louisiana did it for the Who Dats.

Indianapolis quarterback and New Orleans native Peyton Manning wasn't sacked Sunday night nor was he hit very much in Super Bowl XLIV, but he will always remember an Indiana cornerback from Port Allen named Tracy Porter.

Porter delivered the remember-me shot heard around the Who Dat world when he stepped in front of Indianapolis receiver Reggie Wayne — another New Orleans native — to intercept a Manning pass and raced 74 yards for a touchdown to give the Saints their first Super Bowl title in their first try — 31-17 over the Colts.

Manning, the highest-rated quarterback in the fourth quarter this season with seven come-from-behind wins, was on his way to tying the game before just his second interception of the postseason. Porter's touchdown put the Saints up 31-17 with 3:12 to play and virtually ended it.

"He made a great break on the ball," Manning said. "I'm sorry for our fans that I wasn't able to get it done today. I understand how excited the city of New Orleans is going to be."

With Bourbon Street blanketed in black and gold, the traveling Who Dats took over Sun Life Stadium, which is on its eighth name and second in just a few weeks. It might be time for No. 9, at least for a night. Call it Who Dat Way.

The Saints beat the Miami Dolphins, 44-36, here in October when it was Land Shark Stadium after trailing 24-3. Porter returned an interception 54 yards to put the Land Shark on ice in that one. In this one, he put the fun in Sun Life. Porter danced and jumped around the Saints fans who found their way on the field.

"Words can't describe how much this means for New Orleans," Porter said. "I'm a Louisiana native, and this is real big. It means so much. We know the people of New Orleans, the people of Louisiana period — they're behind this team. This team, I have to say this team means more to the people of New Orleans than I can say any team in the NFL."

Saints defensive coordinator Gregg Williams asked for "remember-me" shots on Manning from his defensive linemen and linebackers, but instead he got what the Saints really are. They're not dirty, but they do like to steal.

Porter's touchdown return was the Saints' 10th defensive touchdown of the season — most in the NFL. Manning and the Colts only turned it over once, and Porter made it count.

"It was a close game in the fourth quarter, and we had to be who we are. We get turnovers," said Williams, who in one season turned around one of the league's weakest defenses into its most daring.

"If you're afraid to make quick decisions and take chances in the National Football League, you're not going to be around for long," he said.

Williams blitzed his linebackers on the play, and Manning made the wrong quick decision. Wayne also stopped on his route a little too long.

"As soon as Tracy saw him sit down, he broke for the ball because he knew Peyton was going that way," Williams said.

"I saw him do that, and I jumped the route, and the ball came right into my hands," Porter said. "It was great film study. The coaching staff did a great job of preparing us for that route. When I saw my blockers in front of me and only Peyton and the offensive linemen left, I cut back and ran it in."

And he knew it was over.

"Going up two scores knowing the type of defense we have and the type of clock control offense we have, it was real big," Porter said.

Manning drove Indianapolis down one more time and reached the Saints 3-yard line with time running out, but he could not punch it in.

The final seconds ticked off. Black and gold descended onto the field. Bourbon Street filled back up.

"Now the city of New Orleans can exhale a little bit," tailback Reggie Bush said. "This city needed it. A lot of cities really enjoyed their Super Bowls, but this city needed it for all it's been through with Hurricane Katrina. We did it. It's just unbelievable."

Exhale is one option, but Saints linebacker Scott Fujita had another option.

"I think I'm going to be drunk for about 30 days," he said.

Tight end Jeremy Shockey, a Miami native, had another idea.

"I'm single," he said. "Wink, wink." ✢

....

OPPOSITE: Tracy Porter runs a 74-yard interception back for a touchdown. Porter's score gave the Saints a 31-17 lead with 3:12 left to play. *Brad Kemp/The Daily Advertiser*

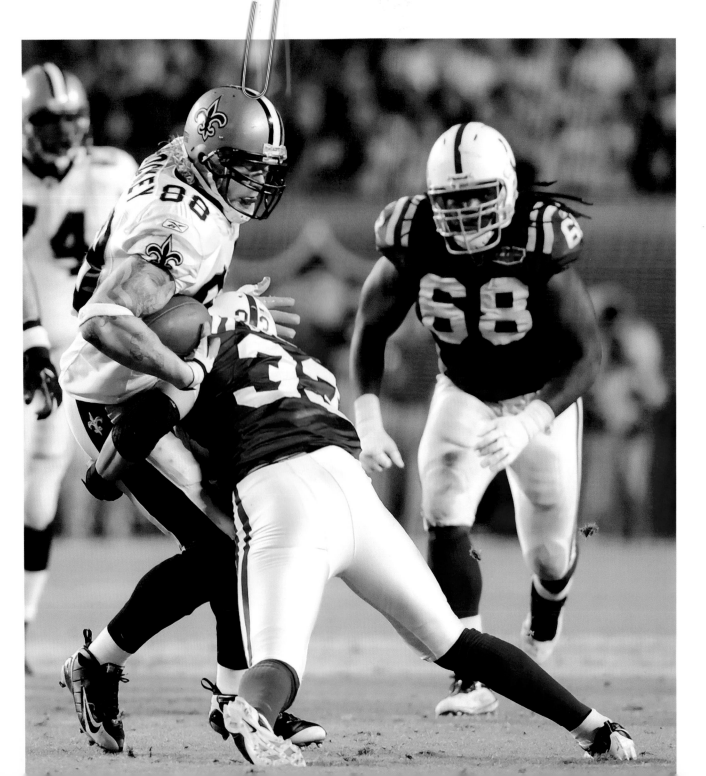

ABOVE: Saints running back Pierre Thomas is tackled by Colts defender Gary Brackett. Thomas scored on a pass from Drew Brees that gave the Saints their first lead of the game in the third quarter. *Brad Kemp/The Daily Advertiser*

LEFT: Tight end Jeremy Shockey battles Colts defender Melvin Bullitt. *Brad Kemp/The Daily Advertiser*

OPPOSITE: Saints running back Pierre Thomas avoids Colts defender Jacob Lacey. *Brad Kemp/The Daily Advertiser*

COLTS COULD NOT STOP COOL HAND OF DREW BREES

By Glenn Guilbeau

Miami — Brees-us was close to perfect.

New Orleans Saints quarterback Drew Brees turned in the second-best passing percentage performance in Super Bowl history Sunday night during a 31-17 victory over Indianapolis.

Brees, who won the MVP honor, completed 32-of-39 passes (82.1 percent) for 288 yards and two touchdowns. The only quarterback better on this stage was the New York Giants' Phil Simms, one of the game's announcers on CBS who was 22 of 25 for 88 percent in his team's win over Buffalo in the 1986 season.

Brees was particularly deadly in the second half, completing 16-of-17 passes for 124 yards and two touchdowns, as he brought the Saints back from a 10-6 halftime deficit.

"The short passing game killed us," Indianapolis safety Melvin Bullitt said. "They didn't go deep. They can't throw it deep. We were moving around fast, and they would dump it off short. We thought they were going to try to go deep, but

they didn't. They adjusted and dumped it off short and got four or five yards here and there, and it worked out well for them. We couldn't get off the field."

Eight receivers caught passes for the Saints, but not one was more than 27 yards. They were short passes, and they were quick.

"In the second half, that ball was going out on a one-two-three-step drop," said Indianapolis defensive end Dwight Freeney, who played despite his injured ankle had the only sack of Brees in the first half. "One, two, three. One, two, three. It was gone. They did a great job of game planning coming out in the second half."

Brees was barely touched in the second half.

"I just think we didn't get to the quarterback enough," defensive tackle Raheem Brock said. "We just didn't get to him using our front enough. I don't think that we attacked them enough. They kept guys in, and they kept us off balance a little bit up front."

....

OPPOSITE: MVP quarterback Drew Brees completed 32 of 39 passes for 288 yards with two touchdowns and no interceptions. Brees did not throw a single interception in the team's three playoff victories.
Brad Kemp/The Daily Advertiser

RIGHT: Instant edition hits the streets Sunday after the win!

Brees also tied the Super Bowl completion record of 32 set by New England's Tom Brady in the Super Bowl XXXVIII win over Carolina.

"He was outstanding, consistent, and he's just a winner," Saints coach Sean Payton said. "He's won it. He's won it for us. I'm just proud of him."

The Saints had no turnovers.

"We took care of the football, converted on third down and scored touchdowns," said Brees, who did not know he won the game MVP until a reporter told him.

"Is it me? It's such a tremendous honor," he said. "But to be a Super Bowl champion is enough for me." ⚜

....

TOP LEFT: Saints defensive coordinator Gregg Williams celebrates after the Super Bowl win over the Colts. Williams' defense held the Colts to seven points in the final three quarters. *Brad Kemp/The Daily Advertiser*

BOTTOM LEFT: Center Jonathan Goodwin celebrates after Jeremy Shockey's score gave the Saints the lead in the fourth quarter. *Brad Kemp/The Daily Advertiser*

FAR LEFT: Saints safety Darren Sharper celebrates after stopping the Colts on a fourth-down play that sealed the win for New Orleans. *Brad Kemp/The Daily Advertiser*

OPPOSITE: Saints fans show the "Who Dat?" theme that became the rallying cry for the team and helped unify supporters of the Black and Gold. Saints fascination gave way to relief to the storm-ravaged city and the championship-starved fans finally saw their dreams come true. *Brad Kemp/The Daily Advertiser*

LEFT: Saints MVP quarterback Drew Brees hoists the Vince Lombardi Trophy into the air after winning the Super Bowl on Sunday, Feb. 7, 2010. "We love you, we love you, baby," Brees said after winning. "The Who Dat Nation allowed us to be here. What you did is you gave us the strength and the courage to know that we could do it. This championship is for you, New Orleans." *Brad Kemp/The Daily Advertiser*

OPPOSITE TOP LEFT: Saints tight end Jeremy Shockey celebrates after the Saints beat the Colts. Shockey's fourth-quarter score gave the Saints the lead in the game. *Brad Kemp/The Daily Advertiser*

OPPOSITE BOTTOM LEFT: Saints owner Tom Benson holds the Saints' first-ever Lombardi Trophy after the team topped the Indianapolis Colts. *Brad Kemp/The Daily Advertiser*

OPPOSITE RIGHT: Head coach Sean Payton celebrates the franchise's first world title in his fourth season with the team. *Brad Kemp/The Daily Advertiser*

SAINTS FANS, WHAT ELSE TO SAY: LAISSEZ LES BON TEMPS ROULER

By Rick Cleveland

MIAMI — When New Orleans finally came marching in 43 years later, the Saints did so with style, substance, the excellence of Drew Brees and the cunning of 46-year-old first-time Super Bowl coach Sean Payton.

It took all that — and more — for the Saints to beat the Indianapolis Colts and New Orleans' own Peyton Manning by a 31-17 score on Sunday in Super Bowl XLIV.

And no, those weren't pigs flying through the air over Sun Life Stadium. That was confetti and fireworks. Today, Satan is freezing. Check the Mississippi River. It might be flowing north. The Saints — the New Orleans Saints, people!!! — are football champions of the world.

Laissez les bon temps rouler! Let the good times roll.

Brees, as usual, was simply magnificent. But the 44th Super Bowl turned on the gutsy halftime

call of coach Sean Payton.

After trailing 10-0 early, the Saints were behind 10-6 at halftime. Payton knew the Saints weren't going to beat Manning by playing it safe. He most certainly did not.

That's why he called for an onsides kick to open the half. The Saints recovered the perfectly executed kick, giving them the jump-start needed to go on and outscore the vaunted Colts 25-7 in the second half.

It was the kind of bold decision Saints fans have come to expect from Payton, who has never been shy about taking chances.

He and Saints general manager Mickey Loomis took one four years ago on Brees' then-wounded right shoulder. The Miami Dolphins, the host team for this Super Bowl, had the first crack at signing the free agent away from the San Diego

···

TOP LEFT: Saints fans wait at the door of Academy Sports in Lafayette, La., to purchase Saints Super Bowl champions T-shirts after the Saints' win. *P.C. Piazza/The Daily Advertiser*

BOTTOM LEFT: Saints fans buy Saints Super Bowl champions T-shirts at Academy Sports. *P.C. Piazza/The Daily Advertiser*

FAR LEFT: Sophia Alison celebrates with the rest of the Saints fans on Bourbon Street in the French Quarter in New Orleans, after their team won their first Super Bowl in franchise history. *Denny Culbert/The Daily Advertiser*

Chargers and passed on him.

Payton and Loomis recruited Brees to Hurricane Katrina-ravaged New Orleans, the first step toward bringing the Lombardi Trophy to New Orleans in this, the 43rd year of the Saints' existence.

BREES IS MVP

Brees completed 32-of-39 passes for 288 yards and two touchdowns to properly claim MVP honors. He out-dueled his good friend, Manning, the four-time NFL MVP. That's all he did.

Afterward, tears streamed down Brees' face as he held his 1-year-old son and surveyed the victory scene and waved to fans.

"We played for so much more than just ourselves," Brees later said. "We played for our city, the entire Gulf Coast region, the entire Who Dat Nation that was behind us every step of the way."

Earlier in the week, ex-Saint Deuce McAllister had assessed New Orleans' chances. "We don't have to play a perfect game to win, but we have to play one of our better games for sure."

He was right. And the Saints

were not perfect, especially not early. They appeared to have predictable first-time Super Bowl jitters. The usually sure-handed Marques Colston dropped what would have been a drive-extending first down pass in the first quarter. Offensive lineman Zach Strief flinched ever so slightly on a second and goal play at the Colts 3-yard line in the second quarter. Even Brees misfired on a couple passes he normally hits with ease.

You can't keep making those kinds of mistakes and beat Indianapolis or Manning. But as flawed as the Saints were early, they were almost perfect over the last three quarters.

Here's perfect:
- No turnovers.
- A defense that got better and better as the game wore on and clinched the victory on Tracy Porter's 74-yard fourth quarter interception return.
- Garrett Hartley's three-for-three on field goals, all of more than 40 yards, the first kicker in Super Bowl history to achieve such a feat.
- Thomas Morstead's powerful punting and kickoffs that helped the Saints control field position.
- And Brees, oh my goodness, Brees. After hitting only three of his first seven passes, he completed 29 of his last 32 passes. That's right: 29

of his last 32.

Most quarterbacks aren't that accurate in warm-ups. And Brees didn't just complete passes, he feathered them into receivers, hitting them in stride, so that they could catch them and keep running.

"Brees' was just magnificent tonight, unreal," Payton said. "He was so efficient."

Like everyone else, Brees was surprised when he learned that the Saints would kick onsides to start the half.

"Who would have thought we would do that at that point in the game?" Brees said, smiling. "It surprised everybody. It was huge."

The onsides kick, the first in Super Bowl history before the fourth quarter (when trailing teams get desperate), was part of the game plan.

"It was something we had seen on film and practiced all week." Payton said. "We knew we would call it at some point, and I told them at halftime we were going to do it and let's go make a play. It ended up being like a turnover."

MANNING KNOWS

In defeat, Manning completed 31-of-45 passes for 333 yards, a touchdown and the one huge interception.

Said Manning, "We had some

chances. Give the Saints all the credit. They made the plays when they had to, and we didn't and that was the difference in the ball game. I know how much this means to the city of New Orleans and all their great fans."

Manning is a guy renowned for his work ethic, particularly his work in the film room. Porter spent some time in the film room, too, these past couple weeks.

Asked about his game-clinching interception, Porter responded, "It was great film study. We knew that on third-and-short, they stack their receivers and they like the outside release for the slant. I got a great jump and made a play."

Porter cut in front of Reggie Wayne, swiped the pass and was never touched.

A native of Port Allen, La., who played his college ball in Indiana, Porter knew how much the victory meant to his region of the country.

"It means so much words can't describe," Porter said.

He's right. Words can't. ✦

TOP FAR LEFT: Saints running back Pierre Thomas holds up a number one to the crowd. *Denny Culbert/The Daily Advertiser*

BOTTOM FAR LEFT: Saints kicker Garrett Hartley plays to the Saints fans during the team's Super Bowl parade. *Denny Culbert/The Daily Advertiser*

TOP LEFT: Saints running back Reggie Bush rides in the Super Bowl Championship parade, February 9, 2010 in New Orleans. The city celebrated the team's first appearance and win of the championship game in franchise history. *Denny Culbert/The Daily Advertiser*

MIDDLE LEFT: Saints head coach Sean Payton holds the Vince Lombardi Trophy over his head for the crowd during the Super Bowl championship parade in New Orleans. *Denny Culbert/The Daily Advertiser*

BOTTOM LEFT: Saints tight end Jeremy Shockey and running back Mike Bell throw beads and chant "Who Dat" back at the crowd. *Denny Culbert/The Daily Advertiser*

OPPOSITE: Saints cornerback Jabari Greer celebrates with the crowd as he rides in the parade with other members of the Saints defense. *Denny Culbert/The Daily Advertiser*

FOLLOWING: The Saints' Super Bowl championship parade rolls along Canal Street, New Orleans. *Denny Culbert/The Daily Advertiser*